SURPRISE ENDINGS

SURPRISE ENDINGS

RON MEHL

MULTNOMAH
Sisters, Oregon 97759

SURPRISE ENDINGS

© 1993 by Ron Mehl

Published by Multnomah Books
a part of the Questar Publishing Family

Edited by Larry R. Libby
Cover design by Bruce DeRoos

Printed in the United States of America

International Standard Book Number: 0-88070-489-6

Unless otherwise indicated, Scripture references are from
The Holy Bible: The New King James Version,
©1984 by Thomas Nelson, Inc.

Scriptures references marked KJV are from
The Holy Bible: Authorized King James Version.

Scripture references marked NASB are from
The New American Standard Bible
© 1960, 1969, 1962, 1963, 1968, 1971, 1972, 1973, 1975, 1977
by The Lockman Foundation.

Scripture references marked NIV are from
The Holy Bible: New International Version
© 1973, 1978, 1984 by the International Bible Society.
Used by permission of Zondervan Publishing House. All rights reserved.
The "NIV" and "New International Version" trademarks are registered in the
United States Patent and Trademark Office by International Bible Society.
Use of either trademark requires the permission of International Bible Society.

Scripture references marked TLB are from
The Living Bible © 1971 by Tyndale House Publishers, Wheaton, Ill.
Used by permission.

Scripture references marked Phillips are from
J. B. Phillips: The New Testament in Modern English, revised edition,
© 1958, 1960, 1972 by J. B. Phillips.
Used by permission of Macmillan Publishing Co., Inc.

93 94 95 96 97 98 99 00 01 02 - 10 9 8 7 6 5 4 3 2

DEDICATION

To my wife, Joyce, who is the only angel I know who lives full-time on this planet. She is the most precious gift the Lord has ever given to me. When the Lord used 1 Corinthians 13 to describe true love, He obviously had her in mind.

To our son, Ron Jr., who has modeled for us in so many ways the goodness of God. His love for the Lord has brought so much joy to our hearts and our home. His suggestions, help, and skill in writing have made my work much easier. I could never thank him enough for his patience and the sacrifice of his time.

To our son, Mark, a gifted young man who has blessed us with much happiness. He has an amazing way of showing us that, when things seem bad, there are many reasons to feel good. His uncompromising love for Christ has been a constant source of strength to us.

ACKNOWLEDGMENTS

Joyce and I would like to acknowledge our parents for always believing in us, for their consistent faith toward God, and for teaching us so many good things. Our utmost thanks to Mr. and Mrs. Carl Cadonau, whose Christian lives have been a source of strength, joy, and blessing, and for making us feel a part of their special family.

To Dr. Jack Hayford, who has encouraged me in so many things, but especially in regard to writing this book. He prodded, encouraged, and prodded some more. For his impact on my life, I will be forever thankful.

My sincere thanks to Dr. Van Cleave, Sandy Gunderson, Dr. Roy Hicks, Jr., Dr. Raymond Cox, and Bruce Farmer, M.D., for their insightful contributions, and especially for the prayers. My heartfelt thanks to Gayle Potter and Debbie Matheny, my secretaries, who worked tirelessly over the course of this undertaking with their normal grace and smiles. I am deeply indebted to them. My thanks to Norma Mueller, whose help and research has contributed so greatly, and Michele Tennesen and Tawny Johnson for their constant encouragement. And to Brenda Josee, who, from the very beginning, believed in me.

I will be eternally grateful to Larry Libby, my editor, for his masterful skill in writing. Frankly, I think he should be everyone's editor. If this book is of any value, it is because of the Lord and Larry. I am a Libby believer. I don't think he could create the world or make the sun shine in Oregon 365 days a year, but the pictures he can create and the emotions he can stir with words, to me, are unparalleled. With deepest affection and gratitude, I say thank you.

Finally, I would like to express my highest regard for the congregation I pastor and the co-workers with whom I am privileged to serve. You have so graciously been used of the Lord to shape my life and show me the goodness of God.

Contents

FOREWORD

You're about to meet a person you'll find impossible not to love. I've known Ron Mehl for thirty years, and he continues to remind me of the Sara Lee commercial... "Everybody doesn't like something, but nobody doesn't like Sara Lee!"

Nobody doesn't like Ron Mehl, either. But there's a reason why this highly principled, steadfast, and godly man is so winsome.

Of all the Christians I've known, he has one of the most unique ways of communicating the love of Jesus Christ. It's hard to define, but it's real. It's not a style of smooth speech, though he's enjoyable to listen to. The fact that thousands flock to hear him every Sunday tells you that. The Beaverton, Oregon, congregation he pastors is attended by more people in a typical week than any other church in the state.

But Ron's loving communication is more than speaking skills. When you've been around him as much as I have, you begin to recognize the key. The love of the Lord comes *through* him extraordinarily simply because he so extraordinarily loves the Lord.

That might sound syrupy to some. But I'm not addressing the maudlin or the sentimental here; nor am I talking some "retreat from reality" order of mysticism. The dimension of love you encounter in Ron Mehl is born of a life which has gone through the fire and come out with a purer, rarer quality. That "fire" is very real: a decade-long bout with leukemia. Amid the flames I've watched this man seem to find "a fourth Man" there, just as the famous Hebrew children of Daniel 3. There's "something special" with him.

There's something special about this book, too.

I saw it the first time Ron told me about a message he'd brought to his congregation, called "Ten Good Things about Bad Things." Through years of friendship we've often "talked shop" together, but mostly we end up "talking Jesus." The reality of Christ Himself is central to the focus of any faithful pastor—that deep desire to see people "connect" with the Savior's *real* life and power. And when I recognized the unusual degree of practical warmth and wealth in the message he had mentioned, I said, "Ron, that *has* to be a book."

He demurred. Characteristically. He tends to withdraw from anything that might give the appearance of "pushing for recognition." The idea of publishing seemed, for him, presumptuous. I crowded in. "Ron, that's a deceiving kind of presumed humility. And I'm challenging it, because I'm telling you—the message is too important to be denied a larger platform!"

Without elaborating the details of the conversation, the book in your hands says it.

I won.

You're about to win, too. Not a sweepstakes. Not a lotto. Man's "win" system is too chancy and deals only in transient resources. God's "good things" are not released by luck or the spin of a wheel. And the rewards they bring are strong enough to infuse a lifetime with meaning and durable enough to lift us into eternity.

Let Ron tell you about it. Believe me, you'll never see "bad things" the same way again.

> Dr. Jack Hayford
> The Church On The Way, Van Nuys, California

CHAPTER ONE

The Last Chapter

I actually know people who refuse to read a book until they've previewed the last few pages. Then, if they're satisfied with the ending, if they're sure in their hearts that Everything Turns Out Right, they'll go ahead and begin at chapter 1. Surprise endings are lost on these folk. They don't like suspense; it makes them nervous. They don't care to wonder; they want to know. If the book has a surprise ending, they want to get it out of the way right off the top so they can relax and enjoy the read.

If you are one of those people, please note that for your benefit I have placed The Last Chapter first. You're reading it now. Without bothering to flip pages, you can read the last three paragraphs and decide if you want to go on. We'll get our surprise ending out of the way right up front so you can kick back, take your shoes off, brew a cup of tea, and enjoy the book.

The very end of the book is this: God delights in taking the Bad Things in our lives and making them into Good Things. For His children, everything indeed Turns Out Right. We all live happily ever after. Surprise! Now...feel free to enjoy the rest of The Last Chapter.

I had a bike, and it was a Schwinn.

It was red, well-worn, and a little rusty. But it was *mine*.

A strange, yet not uncommon characteristic of bikes operated by nine-year-olds is that oftentimes they move very slowly (such as when it is dinner time and your mom is cooking liver and broccoli), yet at other times accelerate so fast they can hardly be seen by the adult naked eye (as when you're headed to your buddy's house with a promise of his mom's fresh-baked chocolate chip cookies).

On this particular day my Schwinn was traveling at chocolate-chip speed due to the fact that my best friend Raymond had just returned from vacation. I was anxious to show him my new handle grips with streamers on them. Suddenly one of the largest rocks I had ever seen outside of a camping trip moved itself directly into the path of my front tire.

Most grown-ups suppose that rocks spend the better part of their days simply lying about in the sun, presumably minding their own business. That is arguably the kind of reputation rocks prefer. But any child will tell you that at a moment's notice rocks can (and do) move right out in front of you (where they weren't before) and trip you up when you're running or—as in my case—

launch your Schwinn into low-level flight.

My reentry was particularly abrupt, and I was forced to eject, resulting in one skinned knee and one bruised ego.

Raymond helped me into his house, and his mom went to work with her favorite remedy for cuts, scrapes, and stings. The salve she used was smooth and minty. The moment she spread it on, my wound felt cool.

But it wasn't the remedy I wanted.

My mother's medicine was a potion called "Mercurochrome," and it was anything but cool and minty. When she daubed that foul orange stuff on one of my cuts it was like pouring on liquid fire. Even the smallest scrape or puncture could be set ablaze. But Mom always assured me the burning meant the medicine was *working*. The bad of the hurt came first; the good of the healing ingredients came later. Since the ointment Raymond's mom applied wasn't hurting, I assumed it wasn't helping.

Mercurochrome helped form my conviction that there are Good Things about Bad Things. You might think starting this book with The Last Chapter is a Bad Thing. Most books, after all, start with The First Chapter. Yet this book begins with the end, because that is precisely where many of us feel we reside. Many of us feel like we're already in The Last Chapter: out of sorts, out of pocket, out of ideas, out of sync, and very nearly out of hope.

It wasn't so very long ago that I faced a Last Chapter. After what I thought was a routine physical, my family doctor called me into his office.

"Ron, the news isn't good. You have leukemia...a slow-moving form of cancer."

He needn't have explained. A pastor friend of mine in Minneapolis had just died of the disease. I knew about leukemia; I just couldn't believe that I had it. It was like someone had grabbed my life's book out of my hands, flipped through the pages, then handed it back to me. And I found myself staring at The Last Chapter—long before I'd ever wanted or expected to. If this was a surprise ending, I didn't want to read it.

Receiving that kind of news is like a punch in the stomach. It knocks the wind out of you. So many things flash through your mind. *Where do I turn? Who do I tell? What should I say? What shouldn't I say?* So many questions. So much confusion. People gather around you to support you in prayer and speak words of faith and hope. Some come with the right remedy at the right time. Others with the right remedy at the wrong time. Still others are just plain wrong.

I've heard of every cure under the sun. I have a file full of them. Everything from jumping into a pool with dolphins to bizarre diets to coffee enemas. Some well-meaning people seem to have the clear word from the Lord for me:

"It's just a test of your faith. A pathway to growth."

"Your problem is a lack of faith."

"There is sin in your life."

"You shouldn't be a pastor."

"You're out of the will of God."

"How can you minister to someone who's sick when you need healing yourself?"

During that first barrage of formulas, cures, counsel, and remedies, I remember a very quiet moment when my wife Joyce and I sat together on the couch in our home. I remember her arms around me.

I said, "How are you doing and what do you think?"

She said, "The servant of the Lord is indestructible until God is through with him."

Her words were a strength to me—a comfort when so many things seemed so wrong. We turned to the Lord and His Word, finding particular encouragement and help in the psalms and the Gospels. We were reminded that peace and rest don't come from understanding everything, but from trusting the Lord with all our hearts even when we don't understand anything.

In this, the biggest Bad Thing of my life, I was beginning to see some Good Things. The Lord's Mercurochrome was still burning in my wound like fire, but it was *working*.

Now you know how the book ends. The catch is, you have to read all the way through to find out how the book *begins*.

God delights in surprise beginnings, too.

CHAPTER TWO

Temptation

Then Jesus, being filled with the Holy Spirit, returned from the Jordan and was led by the Spirit into the wilderness, being tempted for forty days by the devil. And in those days He ate nothing, and afterward, when they had ended, He was hungry. And the devil said to Him, "If You are the Son of God, command this stone to become bread." But Jesus answered him saying, "It is written, 'Man shall not live by bread alone, but by every word of God.' " Then the devil, taking Him up on a high mountain, showed Him all the kingdoms of the world in a moment of time. And the devil said to Him, "All this authority I will give You, and their glory; for this has been delivered to me, and I give it to whomever I wish. Therefore, if You will worship before me, all will be Yours." And Jesus answered and said to him, "Get behind Me, Satan! For it is written, 'You shall worship the LORD your God, and Him only you shall serve.'" Then he brought Him to Jerusalem, set Him on the pinnacle of the temple, and said to Him, "If You are the Son of God, throw Yourself down from here. For it is written: 'He shall give His angels charge over you, to keep you,' and, 'In their hands they shall bear you up, lest you dash your foot against a stone.'" And Jesus answered and said to him, "It has been said, 'You shall not tempt the LORD your God'" (Luke 4:1-12).

Part of the reason they pay professional baseball players so much is to answer worn-out questions from would-be baseball analysts.

I was speaking in Seattle not long ago, when I was introduced to Pete O'Brien, first baseman for the Seattle Mariners.

He probably heard something click in my head as we shook hands.

He probably knew what was coming.

"You know, Pete, there are just one or two *little* things I've always wanted to ask someone like you."

"Oh,...really?"

Pete was gracious. I popped up a few questions and he was willing to field them.

"Do you guys, umm, pretty well know the different pitchers' styles—I mean, what they'll throw in different situations?"

"Pretty well," he said.

"Do they know *you?*"

"Oh, yeah. They know the strengths and weaknesses of every batter they'll face. They know if you're a great fastball hitter, or if you're a terrible curveball hitter."

"They know all that?"

"Oh, sure. They keep a book on everyone—your hitting average, home runs, strike outs, and what pitches you'll swing at in a given situation."

"No kidding!"

"Yeah, and then at the crucial point—when the game is on the line—the pitcher and catcher have a quick summit meeting. The pitcher says, 'I think this guy probably *thinks* I'm going to throw a curveball. He knows that I know he's a terrible curveball hitter. I think he'll be anticipating a curve ball.' Assuming the batter will be looking to guard his weakness, the pitcher decides to go right at the batter's strength, a high fast-ball."

That conversation with my new friend flashed across my mind a few weeks ago as I studied Luke 4.

Two thousand years ago, a lonely Nazarene carpenter stepped up to the plate at a crucial moment. But it wasn't just a game on the line—*everything* was on the line. Your eternal destiny and mine. Salvation for the whole world. Unimaginable implications stretching into endless ages.

What did hell's book of statistics have that day on a famished young Jew named Jesus? With all the forces of darkness cheering him on, what would the pitcher throw at Him?

It would seem prudent that he throw his best stuff. They say, "It's three strikes and you're out." Hell's starting pitcher threw several pitches at our Lord—all designed to challenge the most basic and essential areas of human need. As a result of this head-to-head duel, the potential results of all other battles yet to be waged would be decided.

When it comes to temptation, every person will have his or her time at bat. There are no designated hitters to stand in for us. We all will enter the batter's box alone. Satan is so desperate to win he'll throw whatever it takes to "get us outta there." He doesn't know everything about us, but he does know where we're weak.

In any book about Good Things and Bad Things, temptation has to be one of the *worst* things. Look back through history at the strike outs. From Adam and Eve to King Solomon to Judas Iscariot. Untold horrors—all the incomprehensible evils since the Fall—have occurred when men and women succumbed to temptation.

A very Bad Thing.

But then...Jesus was tempted.

And did not strike out.

And calmly faced the worst hellfire fastballs Satan could hurl and came through it all with power and glory and a rock-hard commitment to walk His Father's path.

And that was a Good Thing. I can't even tell you how good.

So which is it for you and me? Can this most dreadful Bad Thing become for us a Good Thing?

Perhaps the first step to answering that question is to get a better handle on what this phenomenon is all about.

Just what is temptation?

What Temptation Is

Temptation, at its core, is a shortcut.

It's the fast track to quick results. Satan's strategy against Christians usually suggests we do three things: move quickly, think shallowly, and invest ourselves deeply.

When we *move quickly* we are prone to surrender to the unbridled desires of the flesh. The flesh is driven by sudden urges and fleeting passions, not by deliberate convictions.

When we *think shallowly* we don't take the time to weigh and consider the ramifications or consequences of our choices.

When we *invest ourselves deeply* in an action, attitude, or thought pattern it becomes increasingly difficult to withdraw.

Temptation masquerades as better, quicker, and easier, but is in the end a more expensive and painful way. Its offerings are deceptive and always second best. From steroids to premarital sex to cheating on Wall Street, temptation looks, sounds, and feels good on the surface. But beneath its facade, the reward is *short-term* and the consequences are *long-term*.

I've always been drawn by shortcuts. I can recall a summer morning many years ago when Mom called to me from the kitchen just as I was heading out the door with my baseball and mitt.

"Son," she said, "would you please go and dig the dandelions? They're beginning to take over the front yard."

Now I loved my mom and would do anything she asked, but...when you're eleven years old and playing baseball is your dream for the day, the prospect of two or three hours in a dandelion patch is a terrible come-down.

From the field of dreams to a field of weeds.

It was really almost more than a boy could bear.

I dragged myself out the door, flopped down on the front lawn, picked up the knife, and dug up two or three. The pesky things had roots like a redwood. After what seemed like an hour, I looked up to gaze over the yard...a veritable sea of yellow blossoms. There must have been *hundreds* of those things, their little golden heads bobbing in unison to the summer breeze. Despair filled my heart. *This is gonna take all day!* I told myself.

That's when I came up with my short cut.

I simply crawled the length of our yard and pulled off all the flowers. The whole thing hardly took more than twenty minutes. Mom was pleased and impressed.

A few days later, however, a vast ocean of yellow lapped at the front porch and back patio. The dandelions were not only back, they had multiplied ten-fold. And I had some serious explaining to do.

That's the way it is with shortcuts. They rarely deal with the root of the problem. They're cosmetic, and may look good for the moment, but what seems so good ends up so bad.

What Temptation Does

Temptation, like a great crowbar, seeks to lever people away from their God-given responsibilities and bar their way to the Lord's rich and lasting rewards. Ephesians 5 and 6 suggest spiritual warfare rages in predictable places: our responsibilities to our families, our ministries in the church, and our service on the job. It is little wonder we see a breakdown of the family, division in the church, and dissension on the job. If Satan can succeed in prying us away from our personal responsibilities, he creates a gaping hole in God's protective covering over our lives that leaves us—as well as those around us—vulnerable to his attack.

If we really stop and think about it for a moment, Satan often offers us things that are already ours...*if we are willing to wait and trust God for them.* In the wilderness Satan challenged Jesus to prove His power—yet He's the Creator of the universe. Satan offered Jesus prominence—yet He's the King of kings and Lord of lords.

In the beginning, Adam and Eve were blessed with authority, position, and power. God had glorious plans for their lives. Little wonder they were so severely seduced by the devil. Seeing that the forbidden tree was good for food, Eve took of the fruit, hoping it would make her wise. This deadly shortcut cost them their lives, their joy, their relationship with God, and—really more than we can begin to comprehend.

God promised Abraham a son from union with his barren wife, Sarah. But then the patriarch took a shortcut with Sarah's maid, Hagar. Abraham was *still* going to have a son by Sarah. But now he would have to wait ten more years...and deal with the consequences of his impatience for the rest of his life.

Esau was a man who yielded to the desires of the flesh and became its slave so that even his birthright, which was a valuable, precious gift from God, didn't have as much meaning to him as a bowl of stew to satisfy a moment's gnawing hunger.

The voice of the tempter continually whispers, "Take it now...indulge yourself now...get your satisfaction now...make your big play now...grab your pleasure now."

I'm reminded of all the radio and TV commercials that sprout up like so many dandelions between January and April. Lending institutions offer to loan people the exact amount of their tax return. Why? So they won't have to wait for a few weeks to spend it! "Why wait for Uncle Sam's check in the mail?" the announcers ask. "Go out and get that boat now. Take that cruise now. Buy those new clubs now. Build that deck now."

Funny that they never mention the interest rate.

The Ultimate Loan Shark doesn't either. But don't kid yourself. Satan's interest rate is extremely high. It adds up quickly. It compounds daily. Before you know it, he owns you.

I counsel many young people who have listened to the slick ads of the Loan Shark. *You want sex now?* he whispers. *Take it. I'll advance you whatever you want. Enjoy yourself. Go for it. Do it now. Don't worry about my fees. We'll talk about that later on.*

And "later on" is when they come into my office. Broken. Stripped of their innocence. Used up. Rejected. Racked by guilt. Ripped apart by regret. Suicidal.

While sex within the confines of marriage is a proper and pleasurable experience, Satan offers to advance us the erotic pleasures at an *improper* time. And the people I've talked to always discover they've only cheated themselves. When they finally get what they think they wanted, they find it didn't fulfill their needs. They lost far more than they gained.

I know a godly and lovely young woman who struggled with being single. She came to believe that her fulfillment, joy, and contentment would come only through marriage. She looked and looked, waited and waited, with no results. Soon, in her desire to satisfy her need for companionship, she decided that *anything is better than nothing.* So she vowed to marry The Next Available Male.

It was just seven months after her wedding with Mr. Available that she came weeping into my office. "Oh, how I wish I was lonely again!" she sobbed. "It would be a lot better than THIS! I didn't realize how good I had it!"

Most of the mistakes we make happen when we hurry and don't think. That's why the advertising agencies of the world spend billions to determine the best way to approach us. They concentrate on our sexual passions, our curiosity, and need to succeed. Working through our emotions, they prod us to make quick, impulsive decisions.

The world says that the shortest route to personal fulfillment is to discover our deepest desires and satisfy them. But feeding an appetite only makes it crave more! In fact, the Book of Ephesians speaks of uncleanness and greediness in the same breath. It's clear that we can *never* satisfy our own fleshly desires. Just try eating one M&M!

The desires of our flesh may appear at times to be only an innocent trickle. But soon, if fed, they become an uncontrollable torrent. You can't overcome the flesh by saying yes, but only by saying no. As Paul said, "I discipline my body and bring it into subjection" (1 Corinthians 9:27).

The media in the Pacific Northwest recently reported a horrifying accident. A rural Oregon couple was keeping a rare liger in a cage in their garage. A liger is the offspring of a tiger and a lion. Not a tame kitty by any stretch of the imagination. Another family was visiting, and went out to the garage to look at the ferocious animal. For some incomprehensible reason, the visiting parents allowed their twelve-year-old daughter to stray near the cage, and actually reach her arm inside to pet the beast. Instantly the big cat sank its teeth deep into the girl's arm and shoulder *and would not let go.* Everyone was screaming and beating the animal with whatever they could find, but the teeth were clamped down like a bloody vise. It took a bullet through the animal's brain to release its iron grip.

That's our flesh. You cannot coddle and tame it. It's quick and greedy and cruel. It has iron jaws. It hangs on and will not let go.

The flesh is like a wild animal, and you'd be well warned to never turn your back on it. It's unpredictable... you're never sure what it's going to do. It will put up with anything until you mess with its food. The moment you stop feeding it, it rises up.

When you corner a panther and face it head-on, it will lie down like a gentle lamb and pretend the confrontation is no big deal. But never turn your back on it because, if given the chance, it will attack in an unguarded moment. The reason some people don't fall during times of temptation is because they realize they *can* fall. They acknowledge and face the weakness of their own flesh.

Unfortunately, most of us learn by experience. No matter how mature you become, you must always remember your flesh will never be weakened or tamed. It must always be dealt with.

How Did Jesus Handle Temptation?

A good question to ask ourselves when faced with seasons of temptation is this: What was the Lord thinking when He faced such savage testing in the wilderness?

Forty days and forty nights is quite a stretch. That leaves lots of time for thinking. What might have been going through His mind? How did He pass the time? I know what I do. I cry and complain, question and complain, get discouraged and complain. But what might Jesus have done? What did He contemplate?

Isn't it likely He was pondering the work of His Father in the wilderness throughout man's history?

Wouldn't He have recalled how He and His Father, with the Holy Spirit, sent Abraham into the wilderness to the mountain of Moriah with instructions to sacrifice his cherished son, Isaac? Wouldn't He have remembered how Abraham responded without question, believing that if he had to kill his boy God would raise Isaac from the dead? Might not Jesus, in *His* wilderness, have recalled the desolation, loneliness, and agony of that moment?

At bleak, barren Moriah, there had been nothing to distract Abraham from total dependence on God. The test pressed the old patriarch to his limits and beyond. It powerfully sharpened his character, molding him by the hand of the Almighty into a giant of a man, the father of faith.

Second, it's obvious from His answers to Satan that Jesus was meditating on the book of Deuteronomy. Wouldn't He have been thinking about the wilderness wanderings of the Israelites? Wouldn't He have remembered how He and His Father, by the Holy Spirit, had protected and fed and nurtured the Israelites, leading them by a pillar of cloud by day and a pillar of fire by night? Israel's forty-year sojourn in the wilderness was a time of testing—to see whether they would obey God or not. Jesus walked those same sands for forty days—enduring a distilled, concentrated time of satanic testing we can't begin to comprehend.

The wilderness was a place for the awesome revelation of God's power and might. It was a time for all the nations to learn that Jehovah was the true God over all the earth. It was also a time for the demonstration of God's faithfulness to His covenant people. In the face of repeated unbelief and hardness of heart, the world would come to know that even though man may be unfaithful, God remains faithful.

Might He not have remembered how His ancestor David fled into the wilderness to hide from the murderous attacks of Saul? Wouldn't He have recalled the songs of Jesse's son...psalms composed under star-strewn desert skies, in the black depths of limestone caves, or in the shadow of towering rocks in the lonesome afternoons? Can you see His sun-cracked lips moving, silently forming the words through the long hours of testing?

In the shadow of Your wings
I will make my refuge,
Until these calamities have passed by...

For in the time of trouble
He shall hide me in His pavilion;
In the secret place of His tabernacle
He shall hide me;
He shall set me high upon a rock...

You are my hiding place;
You shall preserve me from trouble;
You shall surround me with songs of deliverance.

Certainly Jesus would have found God's Word to be

a pavilion of comfort during those days of pressure and nights of distress.

He would have reflected that the wilderness was a place of security rather than a place of barrenness and death. He would have realized that intense fellowship with His Father in a season of deep trouble and testing was a thing to embrace rather than shun.

One more thing. Could He have been thinking of you and me?

Might He not have thought about the privilege He'd have in the future to encourage us as we face our God-appointed times of testing? If He had not endured during those fierce hours of confrontation with Hell, how could the writer of Hebrews have penned these words?

> Seeing then that we have a great High Priest who has passed through the heavens, Jesus the Son of God, let us hold fast our confession. For we do not have a High Priest who cannot sympathize with our weaknesses, but was in all points tempted as we are, yet without sin. Let us therefore come boldly to the throne of grace, that we may obtain mercy and find grace to help in time of need (Hebrews 4:14-16).

It was a Bad Thing and a Good Thing.

It was the best of times and the worst of times.

It was Hell and Heaven in close proximity.

It was utter loneliness and indescribable fellowship.

Through it all the Lord Jesus experienced the delivering hand of His Father. He experienced a hardening of purpose. When He was finished He would go forth in power and work this same hardening of purpose in the lives of His saints. And, unlike Israel, God's servant of old, Jesus proved Himself faithful to the Lord's purposes.

Jesus knew well how the wilderness in our lives is a preamble to joy and blessing when we trust in Him.

Then Jesus returned in the power of the Spirit to Galilee, and the news of Him went out through all the surrounding region.

It's the power of God that we so desperately need. The Lord's journey on earth took Him to the wilderness. He knew that while none of us are called to live in the wilderness, we may be asked to visit for a season.

Why is the wilderness so important to God? Scripture brims with accounts of the conflicts of men and women in the wilderness and barren lands. The wilderness shows man the truth of who he is. It peels away his pride. Pride is a horrible disease which goes unchecked in this world. Pride convinces man of the strength of his thighs and the maturity of his mind, while blinding him to the strength of the One who has created all things. Pride blinds us all, but the wilderness removes the mask of pride's lying nature and allows man to see himself for who he really is. There is no cure for pride outside of Christ.

It is God alone in His mercy who sends us out into the wilderness to learn again the first principles. He is the Creator of all that is, and in Him and Him alone all creation lives, and moves, and has its being. All creation is utterly dependent upon Him for the life He has granted each of us.

The wilderness of temptation forces me to acknowledge the power and care of the Almighty God.

It's a place without the noise of the many voices that would draw us away from the plan of God for our lives.

It's a place of deep resolution and often where the deep convictions which mold our lives in God take shape and find their expression.

The Lord stands as a sentry watching the comings and goings of the Christian's daily walk. If God has led you to the wilderness, He will provide a way through the temptation. Nothing you face will be more than He knows you are capable of dealing with, even though it may seem so at times.

Have you ever had the opportunity to watch a baseball game played by the deaf? I think you'd find it fascinating. They can't hear, so hollering out positions and instructions just won't work. During the game—especially the crucial moments—you'll see every player on the field fasten his eyes on the coach. The concentration is incredible. Only with their eyes locked on the coach and his hand signals can they be certain they won't miss a key play or muff a personal assignment. They get all their direction and orders from him.

In the same way, we must keep our eyes on our Lord to remain steadfast. If a Bad Thing such as temptation compels us to rivet our attention on Him, it's a Good Thing.

If you have to bat against the devil, you'd best keep your eye on the Coach's box. He knows every pitch.

He's seen it all before.

CHAPTER THREE

Worry

After these things Jesus went over the Sea of Galilee....Then a great multitude followed Him, because they saw His signs which He performed on those who were diseased. And Jesus went up on the mountain, and there He sat with His disciples....Then Jesus lifted up His eyes, and seeing a great multitude coming toward Him, He said to Philip, "Where shall we buy bread, that these may eat?" But this He said to test him, for He Himself knew what He would do. Philip answered Him, "Two hundred denarii worth of bread is not sufficient for them, that every one of them may have a little." One of His disciples, Andrew, Simon Peter's brother, said to Him, "There is a lad here who has five barley loaves and two small fish, but what are they among so many?" Then Jesus said, "Make the people sit down."...Jesus took the loaves, and when He had given thanks He distributed them to the disciples, and the disciples to those sitting down; and likewise of the fish, as much as they wanted (John 6:1-11).

Worry and fear become homogenized in my brain sometimes. But there *are* subtle differences.

When I'm afraid, I know what I'm dealing with. I can put a name to it. Fear of shots. Fear of heights. Fear of rats. Fear of punishment.

When I was very young, I was allowed the run of my yard. Within its boundaries, I was crown prince. I could do just about anything my little heart desired. I could play in the mud. Play ball. Play with the neighbor kids. The street, however, was my boundary line, the end of my world. Beyond this, I had been warned time and again, I must not go.

Or else.

But I decided one day, like all great explorers, that my world simply wasn't big enough. I had discovered its mysteries and delved into its secret places. I knew every rock, bug, weed, and tree limb. But in that great, green, wonderful place called "across the street," there were new trees to climb, new holes to dig, new boards to peer under, and new nooks and crannies to explore. With a short glance behind me to see if Mom was looking, I set off for the great unknown.

It was a brief voyage. What I hadn't counted on was

that Mom was *already* across the street. She had chosen just that moment to go to the mailbox. She saw me before I saw her, and her yell must have carried for miles. I knew from that tone of voice, it wasn't a call for fellowship. It turned my blood to ice. Of course, *the* number-one-of-all-time worst thing to hear your mother say is, "That's it! Go to your room and *wait for your father to come home!*" That's exactly what Mom yelled as she came to get me.

When one's father finally arrives home and walks into the room, looking as big as Goliath, that is *fear*, but the forty-five minutes spent waiting is *worry*. And I worried. I rehearsed in my mind all the possible explanations I could come up with. Then I thought of all my father's possible responses. Finally, I thought of all the theoretical rebuttals I could offer. Sort of like planning chess moves in advance.

When I finally heard my father open the door, I almost felt relieved. Oh, yes, I was afraid of the impending punishment, but the worry was gone. It was out of my hands and into my father's.

Worry seems to be one of those Bad Things we refuse to live without.

When we're in high school, we worry we won't receive the grades or SAT scores to get into the right college.

When we finally reach college, we worry we won't find work when we get out.

Then we worry about finding the right husband or wife with the right looks and the right personality to dwell with us in the right house (in the right neighborhood).

Finally, we worry if we'll be successful enough to

support ourselves in the lifestyle to which we've become accustomed. Only then do some people think they can sit back, take a breath, and declare their worries over.

Then come the children!

Worry is the way I feel when I face a large unknown. I lie in bed at night and try to put shape and substance to it. It stares back at me from the bathroom mirror, colors the sky outside my window, sprinkles itself over my cereal at the breakfast table, carpools with me on the way to work, and waits for me on my desk like an ugly, lumpish paperweight.

I just can't seem to let it go.

Until I share it with Someone Else.

And that—right there—is the very Good Thing about the Bad Thing of worry. We'll talk about that in a moment.

People face their worries in a myriad of ways. Some make poor decisions, some give in to discouragement, some numb their anxieties with alcohol or pills, some get angry, and still others quit, withdraw, or even take their own lives. That's what happens when we allow worry to saturate our minds instead of *dealing* with it: something which seems so benign, simple, and easily managed becomes an uncontrollable monster.

I cannot count the scores of worried people who have come to me during my years as a pastor. While no two problems are alike, there is a common thread: Though rooted in their "yesterdays," their worries center on what may or may not happen in their "tomorrows."

They are desperately worried about the future.

I can tell you what I've told all those I have counseled: There can be no better way to learn to deal with worry than to examine Jesus' life and teaching as a pattern for our behavior.

Try to imagine what it must have been like to have been one of the disciples on the day the Lord decided to feed the multitude with only five loaves of bread and two fish. Grounds for worry certainly existed on that day. Try to separate yourself from the starchy Sunday school images of that scene for a moment and consider the *enormity* of what Jesus proposed that evening. It would be like coming home an hour early one night and telling your wife you've invited the entire Los Angeles Rams football squad over for dinner. An extra box of Tuna Helper and half a bag of day-old bagels just won't cut it.

Oh sure, this amazing Rabbi had turned water into wine and had healed a blind man, but *really*. How could anyone have looked out on up to possibly twenty thousand people and not dropped a jaw when He said, "Where shall we buy bread, that these may eat?" (John 6:5).

Back up a minute. Imagine yourself as Philip, a disciple of Jesus, on that day near the Sea of Galilee. Jesus' beloved friend, John the Baptist, was dead. Murdered. And you've come with the other disciples to tell Him. You've been off on assignment—teaching. Now you've gathered together to be with Jesus in His sorrow. But where is He, by the way?

People are *everywhere*. Up on the hillside. Down by the lake. Shoulder to shoulder on the village streets. How can you ever find Jesus among so many?

As you search for Him, you look into the faces of the people. They, too, are hot and tired. They carry nothing. Their clothes are simple; their sandals are dusty. They've come a long way. Their eyes reveal the anguish and defeat they've come to regard as normal. They, and their father's father's father before them, have known nothing but foreign rule. Assyria. Babylonia. Persia. Greece. Now Rome. Yet somehow they cling to the hope that their promised Messiah will come and redeem their homeland.

Is Jesus the king they seek? Not likely. He carries neither sword nor armor. He has no horse or chariot. Is He the "David" who will fight their "Goliath?" Thus far, He has ignored their political overtures and offered little sympathy. Why, He even included a *tax collector* among His disciples!

Still, they come. Hoping. Wondering. Seeking. The meek and the lowly. The sick and the lame. The discouraged and the despairing. Small numbers at first, then hundreds, now thousands.

As you pass through the moving mural of faces, suddenly you see Him! He seems to know you've been looking for Him. He motions you and the other disciples up a steep mountain path away from the crowd. By now, however, evening has come. Long shadows steal over the landscape. Clouds elbow in from the west and a warm wind paints whitecaps across the water. Jesus looks up and watches the crowd approaching.

You, Andrew, and Peter are from Bethsaida, the nearby village, and you begin to wonder if all these people will seek shelter there for the night. The people are like sheep without a shepherd; Jesus is moved with compassion.

You're standing there shaking your head when He suddenly turns and hits you with The Question.

"Where in the world can we buy bread to feed these people, Philip?"

He might be joking. No…not a chance. He looks at you expectantly and you know He's serious. Your counselor and mentor and Lord has just given you an overwhelming responsibility. He is waiting for an answer. You're on the spot. What can you do? You're *worried*. You look desperately at the other disciples but realize in a flash that no one has resources to put together a feast of that magnitude. What do you say? The words come tumbling out of your mouth.

"Nearly a year's wages isn't enough to buy even one bite of bread for *this* many people!"

Andrew is a little more resourceful. "I saw a lad with five barley loaves and two smoked fish!" Perhaps he remembers the miracle at Cana.

You know the end of the story. Jesus took the tiny parcel of provisions. After giving thanks, He sent the disciples among the crowd to distribute the food. After everyone had eaten their fill, twelve baskets of bread and fish were left for their doggy bags.

Did Philip respond as you would have? Probably so. We do it all the time. We meditate on the problem and not on the Solution. We worry. Why do we do that?

For a moment let's examine some of the major causes of worry which affect our lives:

1. Worry is the result of blurred vision.

We see—but not clearly. Our vision is out of focus. Philip couldn't take his eyes off the impossible dilemma spread out on the twilight hillside beneath him. The logistical problem seemed so huge that he forgot to take a quick glance at the One who posed the question. One look into His eyes would have answered everything.

Don't you realize who I am, Philip? Don't you see that you're standing next to the Creator God? What's a little bread and fish to the One who clothes the world with grain and fills the sea with life? Look at Me, Philip...I'm right beside you!

2. Worry is the result of spiritual amnesia.

Philip had been there at Cana, when the Lord had changed six stone water tanks into six jumbo carafes of vintage wine. He had seen blind eyes opened, the sick healed, the demon-possessed set free, and even the dead raised back to life. But he couldn't seem to bring the reality of those events to bear on the problem at hand. All of us know what happens when we run headlong into trouble. We're knocked silly by the circumstances. We forget who we are, who God is, what He can do, and what He's provided. We have seen Him perform miracles in the past but quickly forget in the face of new adversities.

3. Worry is the result of worldly ambition.

Some people worry because they don't have enough. Others worry because they have so much they're afraid someone is going to try and take it. If you're not happy with a little money, you won't be happy with a lot. If you're not happy as a married couple without kids, you certainly won't be happy with them. Why? Because worry stems from believing that only when I have more will I truly be happy.

True joy and satisfaction, however, are found only in the Lord. He is all that we need. It's like the old saying: "He never truly becomes all we need until we realize He's *all we have.*"

What Can We Learn from Worry?

Worry reminds us to look beyond the hopeless situation before us. Beyond what first meets the eye.

It can reveal our limitations and inadequacies while highlighting His power and provision.

One thing I have learned throughout the course of my sojourn is that the best lessons in life aren't necessarily learned on the best days.

There are some things only the Lord sees; we can recognize the worry in others, but it's often hard to recognize it in ourselves. Maybe that's why He sovereignly arranges circumstances that force out into the open areas of anxiety that we would not ordinarily be able to see.

God allows those spiritual speed bumps in our lives to slow us down. It helps us to see that we still need His help. We can do a lot, accomplish a lot, but we're still utterly dependent upon Him.

Here's an angle you may have never considered: I shouldn't worry because the Lord worries about the right things, at the right time, for the right reason. Okay—I know God doesn't actually *worry* as we do, in the sense of being upset or biting His fingernails. But He certainly thinks about us a lot. Just listen to what He told Jeremiah:

> For I know the thoughts that I think toward you, says the LORD, thoughts of peace and not of evil, to give you a future and a hope. Then you will call upon Me and go and pray to Me, and I will listen to you (Jeremiah 29:11-12).

So if you want to call worry "serious thinking"...

He's worried about sin—that's why He's our Savior and Redeemer.

He's worried about sickness—that's why He's the Great Physician.

He's worried about our daily lives—that's why He's the Good Shepherd.

He's worried about our spiritual growth—that's why He's the Bread of Life.

He's worried about the future—that's why He's the resurrected, everlasting Lord.

And if *He's* worried about the details of my life, WHAT IN THE WORLD AM I WORRYING ABOUT? In a million lifetimes, I could never worry as efficiently, productively, or sublimely as Almighty God! After all, I need sleep, but He can stay up worrying all night. I need to think about other things, but He can keep examining my situation from a billion different angles. I have limited resources to meet my problems and obligations, but no one has ever put a $1,500 limit on *His* Visa card.

Worry is a Bad Thing that wakes me up to the Good Thing of His constant care for me. Sometimes it takes a ridiculous situation (like the one Philip faced) to whack me alongside the head and make me say, "Wait a minute! This is too big for *me*. This is too much for *me*. This is too heavy, too complex, too important, too risky, too loaded for *me*. He's God! He can worry much better than I!"

I once heard someone ask, "Have you ever seen a bird with wrinkles?" I thought, "No, of course not. What reason would a bird have to worry?"

Birds don't struggle with marital, financial, or emotional problems. They don't even have to book their hotel rooms in advance. They aren't little nervous wrecks, always having to debate their next move. Why?

Because they are cared for by the ultimate Bird Watcher who provides for their every need.

> Look at the birds of the air, for they neither sow nor reap nor gather into barns; yet your heavenly Father feeds them. Are you not of more value than they? (Matthew 6:26).

Wouldn't it be wonderful if we could see our lives from His eternal point of view for a moment? How much He has done for us! How much He is willing to do because of His love!

My mind wanders back to a hot day some time ago. I was playing golf with three close friends. The temperature was clawing its way toward the one-hundred-degree mark, and the humidity wasn't lagging far behind. At that moment our minds weren't on playing the ninth hole, but on the cold-as-a-mountain-spring-dripping-with-ice cola that was waiting for us in the clubhouse at the turn.

Then, out of the corner of my eye, I saw him. He couldn't have been more than four or five years old. His mother was watching him at that discreet *you-can't-see-me-but-I'm-here-watching-you* distance that mothers have down so well. His chubby cheeks were flushed and dripping with sweat.

He was selling Kool-Aid. And, pardon me, but it was very un-Kool, as there was no ice apparent in any of the four cups sitting on top of his large, unshaded rock. I noticed the few paper cups he did have looked—well, a little *used*.

I noticed he didn't wear the friendly grin that so often adorns the faces of people who work in sales. From the looks of things, he hadn't had a lot of takers.

"Hi, son," I said. "How's business?"

"Not too good," he replied.

I looked down at his pitiful little face and felt sorry for him. I, too, have been a Kool-Aid salesman. I decided to do whatever I could to get him out of the sun as soon as possible.

"Are you going to close up shop soon?" I asked.

A somewhat pained expression crossed that sun-burned face, but it was quickly replaced by clenched teeth and a look of determination.

"Nope," he replied.

"Son, how much Kool-Aid do you have left?"

"Four cups," he said, eyeing me and my three companions. He was certainly old enough to count.

"And how much will four cups cost me?"

"Twenty-five cents a cup."

"Well then, I guess I'll take all that you have."

He looked at me. Shocked. This was more than he could possibly have hoped for.

I handed him a five-dollar bill, which was all I had.

"Keep the change, son."

He immediately turned tail and ran.

"Mom!" he yelled. "Mom! I sold all my Kool-Aid!"

As it ended up, I felt good, he felt good, and my friends felt good. They not only received free cups of warm cherry Kool-Aid, they also earned the privilege to buy my Coke and hot dog at the clubhouse because I didn't have any money left.

That little incident has come back to me as I've wrestled with this thing called worry. When you think about it, that's what the Lord has promised to do for all of us. When we're worried or troubled, He comes alongside and purchases all of our Kool-Aid. He knows what we need, and comes to provide it at just the right time— His time. Remember, however, that His time may be before, during, or after our long and difficult day: 1) He told Noah that it would rain long *before* it did. 2) The Lord chose to come to the three Hebrew children (Shadrach, Meshach, and Abednego) right in the *middle* of their encounter with the furnace. 3) Finally, He chose to come to Mary and Martha *after* the death of Lazarus.

Whether it's before, after, or during our trouble, the point is don't worry...He will come. I can only imagine the many times God did good things for me when I never knew it. Personally, I plan to spend a good portion of my time in heaven having God rehearse for me those times that He spared my life, paid my bills, protected me from harm,...and drank my warm Kool-Aid.

After I graduated from high school, I decided to go on to college and study for the ministry. I settled on L.I.F.E. Bible College in Los Angeles. I didn't know anyone there and I'd never really been out of town before, so I worried about going to such a big city.

I'm from a family of nine, and my folks had barely enough money to get by, let alone pay for my college education. Nonetheless, they encouraged me. They put me on a Greyhound bus to L.A. and handed me fifty dollars. It was all they could give. As I boarded the bus—just eighteen years old and going to a place I had never been, to meet people I didn't know—my mom said, "Son, I love you very much and I'm going to pray for you every day. So don't worry; the Lord will take care of everything you need."

My mom, a godly woman, had gained wisdom over the years that led her to look to the Lord as the solution. But I was young and untested. As I gazed out the window and the landscape rolled by, I began to worry about what I would do when I got there, where I would work, where I would live, how I would survive.

Not comprehending the vast distances in a city like L.A., I took a taxi from the bus terminal downtown, all the way out to the college. It cost me twenty-three dollars—almost half the money I had. Even though I was three days early, they let me stay in the dorm.

Registration day was quickly approaching. The problem was I had no job, no money, no friends, and one third of my school bill was to be prepaid before I could even begin classes. I knew I'd probably have to go back home. I went outside and sat alone on the steps of the dorm, feeling heartsick, thinking about home, my mom, and what I was going to do.

As I sat there, I noticed a distinguished-looking man walking across the campus. I discovered later he was Dr. Hall, the college dean. He came over, stood next to me, and said, "Son, your name is Ron Mehl, isn't it?"

"Yes, sir."

"What are you doing?"

"Oh...just thinking."

I realize now that old Dr. Hall probably knew exactly what I was thinking about. We talked awhile about school, and about the things of the Lord. Then he said, "Ron, I'm really glad you're here. I've been the dean a long time, and it never ceases to amaze me how the Lord brings young people like you to school, and then seems to provide for them everything they need."

Could he have known the confusion and turmoil I was going through? Could he have known about the big lump I felt in my throat and how worried I was about tuition? Maybe, maybe not. But the Lord knew.

"Ron, I have some good news for you," Dr. Hall said. "A basketball scholarship has been provided for you. You won't need to pay anything when you register today."

At that moment, my mother's tender words came flooding back to me: *"Son, I love you very much and I'm going to pray for you every day. So don't worry; the Lord will take care of everything you need."*

He did.

He always will.

And He doesn't mind drinking warm Kool-Aid.

CHAPTER FOUR

Storms

Immediately Jesus made His disciples get into the boat and go before Him to the other side, while He sent the multitudes away. And when He had sent the multitudes away, He went up on the mountain by Himself to pray. Now when evening came, He was alone there. But the boat was now in the middle of the sea, tossed by the waves, for the wind was contrary. Now in the fourth watch of the night Jesus went to them, walking on the sea. And when the disciples saw Him walking on the sea, they were troubled, saying, "It is a ghost!" And they cried out for fear. But immediately Jesus spoke to them, saying, "Be of good cheer! It is I; do not be afraid." And Peter answered Him and said, "Lord, if it is You, command me to come to You on the water." So He said, "Come." And when Peter had come down out of the boat, he walked on the water to go to Jesus. But when he saw that the wind was boisterous, he was afraid; and beginning to sink he cried out, saying, "Lord, save me!" And immediately Jesus stretched out His hand and caught him, and said to him, "O you of little faith, why did you doubt?" And when they got into the boat, the wind ceased. Then those who were in the boat came and worshiped Him, saying, "Truly You are the Son of God" (Matthew 14:22-33).

"When you're covered by His wings,
it can get pretty dark."
—Corrie ten Boom

There are two kinds of airplane flights. One you could call "a trip." The other you might call "an experience."

When you board a 737 from Portland to Dallas, pick up a newspaper on the way in, sip a Diet Coke, watch a movie, eat a hot meal, grab a half-hour nap, and hardly sense you've left the ground...that's a trip.

However, when you board a seven-seater (including the pilot and the man employed to hold the door closed) flying from Vancouver, B.C., to Victoria Island into the mother-of-all-storms, that is an *experience.*

I found myself in the latter situation as I traveled to a Canadian pastors' conference. The wind was blowing *east* at 80 miles an hour. We were heading *west*, and our plane had a top speed of 120 miles per hour. As the pilot sat on the taxiway pondering the question, "Is it prudent to take off?" I did a little pondering of my own. Flying at 120 miles per hour against a head wind of 80…would net us a speed of 40 miles per hour. Our plane would be traveling very low (did I mention it was unpressurized?) over the ocean into the teeth of a Pacific storm. At a top speed of 40.

"Prepare for takeoff," came the voice in the speakers.

You have to be kidding! came the voice in my head.

Not long after we lifted off the runway, the high winds and extreme turbulence began taking their toll on our "seven-seater seven." Since I've traveled quite a bit, I'm familiar with the purpose of the little white bags placed in each seat back. But I'd never seen them *used* before.

This time I did.

It's one thing to *see* people using their little white bags. It's another thing to *hear* them being used—all around you, in stereo. It's a humbling experience. In such close quarters, there's no room for machismo. You're forced to abandon all pride and inhibitions and make a decision based on what is best for your body.

As the pilot announced we were nearing the landing site, my thoughts diverted from the distress of those around me to my own fear of the storm.

Is there ever a "right time" for a storm?

We may try, but we can't determine when they will come. Nor can we determine their duration, severity, or effects. We can't control or contain them. For a period of time during our fearful flight I actually thought we might not make it. I even went so far as to point out to the Lord that I still had a lot of shepherding to do and that it might be hard to explain to my wife, sons, and the church I pastor exactly why I had been taken home to heaven while in the middle of doing the Lord's work.

During those moments of personal reflection, I was reminded of a story I had heard about one flight attendant who had to sit in her jump seat and watch the reactions of frightened people as the captain announced that passengers should tighten their seat belts and prepare for a crash landing.

Through the skill of the pilot and the grace of God, however, the plane managed to land safely. When the flight attendant arrived home, she told her pastor about the ordeal.

He was curious. "As you watched the people," he asked her, "what do you think they were doing?"

She looked at him with a wry smile. "I think they were making deals with God." She added, "It felt so good to sit there in peace, knowing I didn't have to make any deals."

The Good Thing about my incredibly bad trip through the Pacific storm was that it taught me something about myself and something about the Lord. You'll see what I mean in a few pages.

Everyone faces fear sometime or another.

In Matthew 14:22-33, Jesus sent His disciples across the sea, and then went up on the lonely slopes of the mountain to keep an appointment with His Father. The men had no idea *they* were about to keep an appointment with a killer storm.

Rowing a fishing boat through a raging Sea of Galilee is the first-century equivalent of flying through severe air turbulence. What's the difference if you're *on* the waves or flying *over* them? The basic ingredients are still the same: You're sick. You're frightened. You're helpless. You're in deadly danger. You're at the mercy of the elements. You're yearning for solid ground beneath your feet.

At least when you're in an airplane the engines are doing all the work. At sea in a fishing boat, you *are* the engine. It's you and your little paddle versus screaming wind and boiling sea. The disciples had been at the oars for hours. When did Jesus send the five thousand away and bundle His men into the boat? Seven P.M., maybe? And when did He come out to them on the water? Some time between 3:00 A.M. and 6:00 A.M. That's at least eight hours hauling on those sticks. And where were they? A long way from either shore.

So in addition to worry and fear and nausea and despair, add *exhaustion* to the list. Maybe you know what that's like. Sometimes the worst thing about enduring storms is feeling so utterly tired. Bone-weary. As if you could just lie right down on the floor and sleep for a week…only you can't. Events won't allow it.

So they've labored all night and it's now sometime before dawn. The blackest hours of all. For sheer desolation of the soul, midnight is nothing compared to "the fourth watch of the night." It is during these predawn hours that lamps burn lowest, darkness lies most heavily, and the spirits of wakeful men sink to their lowest ebb. It's during these hours that the enemy whispers, *Why not just give up? You'll never make it. You'll never get out of this. This is too much for you. Why not just lay down your oar and let the boat go under? Why not get it over with?*

Just when the men in the boat began to listen to this black voice, they caught sight of something...out in the water...out of the night. A wisp of cloud? Sea spray? A sail? Some kind of debris? But how could it be moving against the wind? And why did it look like something *walking?*

Before you write these guys off as superstitious cry-babies, picture yourself in an airliner. In a storm. In the night. With raindrops exploding against your little window. And out over the wing, in the swirling clouds, illumined by the pale blinking lights under the wing...you see a form. Its clothes are whipping in the wind. It's coming closer. It's reaching toward your window.

You say out loud, "Lord, if it's really You, command me to come to You out on the wing!"

The figure motions you to come, and you put your hand on the emergency exit door....

Now that's fear. But somehow—in a flash of time—this biblical account transitions from a story of fear to a story of faith. And hidden within that transition is the secret of how Bad Things such as storms and fear become Good Things in our lives.

As serious and sobering as my wild plane ride over the Pacific may have been, I found myself comforted by six short, momentous words from a psalm.

It was David's cry of faith in Psalm 31:15:

"My times are in Your hand."

At that moment, on that plane, in the middle of that storm, the Lord personalized that Scripture to me. It was as if He was saying, "Ron, YOUR times are in My hand."

Times of fear bring us face to face with God. They remind us that He has promised to be a shelter in the time of storm. Psalm 61:3 says, "For You have been a shelter for me." Isaiah 25:4 says that God is a "refuge from the storm."

The book of Psalms says He's certainly all of that and more. He's my: King (2:6), Glory and the lifter of my head (3:3), God (3:7), Righteous God (4:1), Lord (16:2), Strength (18:1), Rock (18:2), Fortress (18:2), Deliverance (18:2), Shield (18:2), Stronghold (18:2), Support (18:18), Savior (18:46), Redeemer (19:14), Shepherd (23:1), Light (27:1), Salvation (27:1), Help (30:10), Hiding Place (32:7), Delight (43:4), Refuge in times of trouble (59:16), Loving God (59:17), Strong Tower (61:3), Deliverer (70:5), Father (89:26), Portion (119:57), and Comfort (119:76).

The fact is, apart from storms in my life, I never would have taken time to think through these truths about who my Lord really is. Sure, I might have led a Bible study on the "names of God" or quoted that string of verses in a sermon, but I never would have brought the rock-firm reality of Who He Is into the heart of my experience.

How do I know He's my Fortress until, with arrows flying all around me, I run with all my heart into His open gates?

How do I know He's my Hiding Place until I hear the enemy crashing in the brush behind me, feel his breath on the back of my neck, and cry out for a place of refuge?

How do I know He's my Portion until all I treasure and hold dear is suddenly threatened or taken from me?

How do I know He's my Father until I feel orphaned and abandoned and left alone in the storm?

How do I—like Peter—learn that He is my Deliverer until I step out of the boat and plant my foot on fifty fathoms of frothy sea?

As long as I dodge life's storms and stroll down the sunny side of Tranquility Lane, I will never know much about the provision and comfort of God at all. Nor will I care. The fact that my times are in His hands will mean very little to me.

Personal storms disclose a great deal about our inner makeup...perhaps more than we would wish to reveal. As a pastor, I've been called upon to spend time with people who were facing death—but who didn't know the Lord. I've watched fear move across their faces like a living thing. I've had to gather two young children around me and tell them their parents had been killed in an auto accident. I've counseled a young couple who filed for bankruptcy, and lost their home and their jobs. I have shared in peoples' times of fear, trouble, and death.

What I've learned about those experiences is that storms expose an individual's philosophy of life. For some it is nothing more than, "Eat, drink, and be merry for tomorrow we die." For others it's, "Travel the world, get all you can, and do all you can." And then there are those who lead negative, hopeless lives. Their philosophy is, "Keep your nose above the water. Just try to survive."

The fact is, you really don't *know* your philosophy of life until you're forced to open it—like an umbrella in the middle of a sudden storm. You may *think* you're trusting in the Lord, but the howling winds and slashing rain may reveal otherwise.

I believe the only philosophy worth embracing is one that works in death as well as in life. Paul said, "For to me, to live is Christ, and to die is gain" (Philippians 1:21).

The funeral of a loved one or the bedside of a dying friend are difficult places to realize your personal life-philosophy is full of holes.

What Storms Can Teach Us

Storms may sweep down upon us from different directions and for different reasons. Sometimes Satan causes the storm. Sometimes people cause the storm. Sometimes I cause the storm. And sometimes the Lord sends the storm. But no matter who or what the cause, they all work to reveal the same things:

the nature of my faith;
the strength of my commitment;
the level of my maturity;
the health of my attitude;
the measure of my teachability.

God uses many vehicles and tools to teach people lessons, develop their faith, encourage their hearts, and show His power. His track record is trustworthy, and the Word is a treasury of examples that reveal the Good Things about bad storms.

Let's take a closer look at some specifics of what storms in our daily lives can mean.

Storms are times of revelation.

Just as howling winds topple trees with shallow roots, storms underscore areas of our lives that need attention and growth. If you've ever experienced a hurricane, monsoon, or tornado, you know that storms can be very revealing—if only to show us where our roof leaks!

Storms also underline our need of a hiding place. As one born and raised in Minnesota, I can tell you that the best place to be in a storm is the northwest corner of the cellar. As a Christian, I can tell you I've found my hiding place to be the unmovable, unchangeable, uncompromising, eternal wall of God's Word.

Fear not, for I am with you;
Be not dismayed, for I am your God.
I will strengthen you,
Yes, I will help you,
I will uphold you with My righteous right hand
(Isaiah 41:10).

Storms are times of restoration.

We live in a skin-deep world that emphasizes clothing, fashion, makeup, plastic surgery, tummy tucks, and nose jobs. Although there may be nothing wrong with any of these, they are all just cosmetic. Character and substance are shaped in the crucible of adversity. When someone tells me they have no problems and never go through anything difficult, I can say with confidence that I am looking at a shallow person.

Storms always leave us with a list of things to clean up and fix. They are times when God restores to us the things we've lost through negligence, ignorance, rebellion, or sin. For the Christian, storms are a no-lose proposition. They help me to see and acknowledge the loose shutters, missing shingles, and rotten fence posts in my life, while turning me back to the only One who can make the necessary repairs.

Storms are times of maturation and growth.

Someone once told me that the times when plants grow the most are not necessarily during the warm, gentle rains or beautiful summer days. In fact, when the fierce winds blow and the raging storms come is the time of most growth. Botanists tell us that if you were to take a cross-section of the earth during a vicious storm, you could literally observe the roots reaching further down into the soil. The German poet Goethe said, "Talent is formed in solitude, but character in the storms of life."

Bob Weaver, a man in our congregation told me about how his son had awakened one night very fearful, crying out for his mom and dad. Bob went in and sat down at his bedside.

"What's wrong, son?"

"I'm afraid something's going to get me!"

"Son, there's no reason to be afraid. The Lord is here and He's promised to care for us. He also said He'd never leave us, so there's no need to be afraid."

The boy then asked, "Dad, will you pray for me?"

Bob looked at him and said, "No."

At this point, as Bob was telling me the story, I was shocked and even angered by this. I said, "Why in the world did you say that?"

"We love and pray for our children," he said, "and we believe God will guard and protect them. But I refuse to fight *all* their battles or do *all* their praying for them. We want our kids to learn to pray on their own during times of spiritual attack. Then, when they're older and on their own, they'll know how to fight and they won't be fearful."

I've concluded that many kids have little or no capacity to walk in victory when they leave home because a loving, protective parent has always done their fighting for them. As a result, when they face the enemy alone and on his terms, they usually lose.

People ask me all the time how a child can grow up in a Christian home and then turn his back on the Lord. My answer is that, in the midst of his storms, others did all the fighting for him.

Presuming that storms in our lives really are more of a Good Thing than a Bad Thing, how can we position ourselves to gain as much benefit as we can from those inevitable tempests that come screaming down across our placid little lakes? Let's consider several adjustments to our personal posture.

1. Learning from storms requires a decision.

We need to settle in our hearts—in advance—the conviction that God will not let anything touch our lives but that it will reveal sin, facilitate growth, or lead us to repentance. Learning from storms requires trust. The ways of God are often misunderstood, but when we understand Him, we don't have to understand anything else.

2. Learning from storms requires dedication.

God has a plan, a purpose, and a timetable by which He works. Resting in that requires a firm commitment to persevere when others don't. Dedication requires a continual commitment to be teachable, patient, trusting, obedient, and thankful.

3. Learning from storms requires humility.

We can't do everything by ourselves. We need to candidly admit that—to ourselves and to others. The disciple who crawled out of that boat to walk on the stormy sea reminds us that "God gives grace to the humble.... Therefore humble yourselves..." (1 Peter 5:5-6). Peter discovered that even though his heart was right and his zeal unparalleled, there were things in his life only God could do. Humility isn't something done to you, but *something done by you.* This is very important to keep in mind. And while I believe that we must choose to be humble, I also believe that if we fail to make this choice God can and does teach us humility in His own way. God lets you face pressing circumstances "to humble you and test you, to know what was in your heart, whether you would keep His commandments or not" (Deuteronomy 8:2b).

4. *Learning from storms requires living with a sense of destiny.*

People who successfully face life's storms keep their eyes on the larger picture. Storms are only one part of God's scheme for our lives. People who live with a sense of personal destiny find themselves so concerned with fulfilling their call that the enemy has a difficult time side-tracking them with adversity and trouble. People determined to fulfill God's destiny for their lives still have to deal with hard times, but needn't be defeated by them. Our Lord Himself experienced a "divine interruption" to come to earth. He knew it was only one event, albeit a momentous one, in the scheme of God's eternal purpose and plan.

5. *Learning from storms requires the prayers of saints and supply of the Spirit.*

Paul said of his imprisonment:

> I will continue to rejoice, for I know that through your prayers and the help given by the Spirit of Jesus Christ, what has happened to me will turn out for my deliverance (Philippians 1:18b-19, NIV).

It is important to remember that others are praying for us, especially in times of storms. The "help given by the Spirit" is the picture of a movie producer who takes full responsibility for the total funding of the project. The movie may horribly fail or incredibly succeed, but he has chosen to underwrite the endeavor in its entirety. Paul is saying that God, in like manner, has made available to us all of the resources necessary for our deliverance, safety, and personal care.

I would like to conclude with a painless test. Have you ever put your finger in one of those machines that checks your blood pressure for a quarter? Well, I have a little quiz of my own, which relates to Good Things and Bad Things—and storms in particular. Ready? Answer the following questions yes or no. You may give yourself two points for a yes answer, one point for a no answer.

Do you think there is any storm that touches your life that God doesn't know about? Yes ___ No ___

Do you think there is any storm that touches your life that God can't handle? Yes ___ No ___

Do you think there is any storm that touches your life that doesn't have a purpose? Yes ___ No ___

Do you think there is any storm that touches your life that shouldn't teach you something about you? Yes ___ No ___

Do you think there is any storm that touches your life that shouldn't teach you something about your Lord? Yes ___ No ___

All done? If you scored more than five points, then you probably are not trusting the Lord as completely as you should when it comes to your fears. Remember that storms are a learning experience, not God's tools to beat us into submission. Learn to see His goodness, faithfulness, and provision for your life, and rest easily in His promises.

Then fasten your seat belts. It could get a little bumpy before final touchdown.

Count on it.

CHAPTER FIVE

Limitations

On the third day there was a wedding in Cana of Galilee, and the mother of Jesus was there. Now both Jesus and His disciples were invited to the wedding. And when they ran out of wine, the mother of Jesus said to Him, "They have no wine." Jesus said to her, "Woman, what does your concern have to do with Me? My hour has not yet come." His mother said to the servants, "Whatever He says to you, do it." Now there were set there six waterpots of stone, according to the manner of purification of the Jews, containing twenty or thirty gallons apiece. Jesus said to them, "Fill the waterpots with water." And they filled them to the brim. And He said to them, "Draw some out now, and take it to the master of the feast." And they took it. When the master of the feast had tasted the water that was made wine, and did not know where it came from (but the servants who had drawn the water knew), the master of the feast called the bridegroom. And he said to him, "Every man at the beginning sets out the good wine, and when the guests have well drunk, then the inferior. You have kept the good wine until now!" This beginning of signs Jesus did in Cana of Galilee, and manifested His glory; and His disciples believed in Him (John 2:1-11).

When all the planning, counseling, preparing, and rehearsing are said and done, deep down there persists the feeling that no one is *ever* in control of a wedding.

Any number of things can go wrong. Invariably, many of them do.

One of the most memorable weddings I've performed was also one of my first. Things were going along smoothly until it came time for exchanging vows.

I smiled down at the little ringbearer.

"May I have the rings, please?"

As he looked up at me his cherubic expression turned sour and his little lip started to quiver. He began to cry and ran straight for his mother, throwing the rings under the pews about eight rows back.

What was I to do? Yell? Chase after him?

After some coaxing from his relatives and the

promise of a Snickers bar from my office, he crawled under the pews to retrieve the rings, and the ceremony was completed.

I recall another occasion a few years later. It was a classy wedding. All the bells, whistles, and trimmings. In my peripheral vision, I noticed the best man's face. It was an unusual shade of pale green. I remember saying to myself, *He won't be with us for long.* I hoped he could remain vertical for just a few more moments. Then he could collapse at his leisure. As I turned to address the bride and groom, however, I noticed motion out of the corner of my eye. He had disappeared over backward, taking two groomsmen and a stack of flowers with him.

Again, what do you do if you're the preacher? Stop and pray over him? Let him lie there and hope someone has smelling salts handy?

We never covered stuff like that in Bible college. Nor did we discuss what to do when a wedding soloist sings a fourteen-minute medley in the key of C, while the musicians play on in the key of F. Or where to turn when the flowers catch fire during the most tender moment of the ceremony.

Performing weddings has helped me discover a wide range of situations in which I am absolutely limited and inadequate. When it comes to stature, intellect, experience, and skills, preachers—and most everyone else I can think of—were not created equal. We do, however, have one thing in common. It's the "L" word: Limitations.

All we have to do to be reminded of our limitations is to look around. One quick glance will reveal someone who is prettier or smarter or wiser or richer or thinner. Whether it's looks, parentage, position, or power, all of us lack someplace.

Have you ever wondered what our world would be like if we "had it all?"

Would we see beauty in the usual and the ordinary? A sunset? A meadow filled with wild flowers? A cool glass of water on a hot afternoon?

If there were no rain, could there be rainbows?

If we had no questions, would we exercise our minds and search for answers?

If there were no darkness, would our pulse quicken at the first light of morning?

If we were never lost, could we know the relief and elation of being found?

If we were never empty, could we know what it's like to be filled?

If we had no shortcomings, could there be overcomings?

One of my best friends is Brian, a Down's syndrome boy in our church family. Every Sunday after the service, he's the first one on the platform. He attacks me with a long, warm hug, then looks into my face and says, "Passor (meaning pastor), do you love Jeeezuz? I luuuv you!" His simple, undiluted love overwhelms me. He has taught me that love isn't in how much you have to give, but in that you give all you have. Brian will never be an electrical engineer or a brain surgeon, but he does understand that God has made him unique, and that a world full of love comes from giving love away.

Pastors deal with limitations almost daily. I've spent enough hours with enough hurting people to know there are times when there *are* no answers. There are times when things *are* hopeless. There are times when we *are* at a dead end. God allows such times to illustrate the utter helplessness of man and, more importantly, to reveal His own overwhelming sufficiency.

That's what the miracle in John 2 is all about. I've always wondered about that first miracle. Why Cana? Why a wedding? Why wine? It seems like the Son of God could have launched His earthly ministry with something...well, a little more stunning. You know—some kind of celestial fireworks in front of a large crowd or a big group of influential types, with all the cameras rolling. Some kind of first-century sound bite.

It would be easy to get side-tracked searching for some deep, mystical meaning in this little village ceremony. When we're all done picking through the text for ethereal truths, however, we're left with one rather simple and obvious message.

God loves to help people in need.

These newlyweds ran out of refreshments for their reception, and God knew their predicament. One might think, *Everyone runs out of refreshments. What's so special about this wedding?* In that culture, however, to run out of drink would have been an extreme embarrassment to the family name. Because of God's love for us, He cares for even the littlest of things. In light of their crisis He chose to let the miraculous earthly ministry of His Son begin in a setting that would reveal His love for people and establish His commitment to marriage as a priority.

At each and every wedding ceremony I perform, I remind the couple of the miracle of the wedding at Cana. One of the reasons I do this is because I believe that a couple who experiences God's love, grace, and blessing should, in the very beginning, acknowledge their need for a constant flow of God's strength and cleansing power.

After pronouncing the couple man and wife, I turn to their family and friends and announce that as their first official act of marriage the couple has chosen to take communion, even before the traditional "You may kiss the bride."

The bread is representative of the strength we receive from the Lord when we face times of trouble. The cup is representative of the blood of Christ which cleanses us of our sin, impurities, and failures.

Communion reminds the newlyweds that in marriage (just as in their personal lives) there are some things only the Lord can provide. At the very genesis of their marriage, they are inviting the Lord to be a part of their home. They are welcoming the Lord to come and provide for them from Day One what they never could.

Then, as the second official act, the husband does get to kiss the bride.

What was the bottom line of the miracle at Cana? Jesus encountered a distressing human shortfall and proved Himself both able and willing to graciously meet the need through His own creative power.

It's not uncommon for the Lord to use our limited resources to do unlimited things. He used the jawbone of an ass to crush an army. He used a common shepherd's staff to confound the Pharaoh of Egypt. He used a king's insomnia to save Esther—and then her whole nation. He used five hunks of bread and two puny fish to feed a mountainside of hungry campers.

At Cana, all Jesus asked for were six pots of plain water. That was it. He didn't ask for Perrier and a single twist of lime. Just six earthenware jars full of H_2O. Nothing fancy. Nothing else. When He sets His mind to pour out His blessing on someone, any old pot will do.

The church I pastor is blessed with many talented teachers, workers, and servants. Sandy is one of them. I've been her pastor for many years, and have watched her grow in the Lord. It wasn't too long ago that Sandy was totally overwhelmed by her limitations. When I met her, she was a shy, quiet woman with no sense of self-worth, self-confidence, or joy. She could hardly meet my eyes. Life had used her up. Even though I knew there was tenderness and love deep down inside, from the outside she appeared only a shell of a woman. Her life, she felt, was in free fall. She had hit the bottom of some black abyss and couldn't even move—let alone crawl out. There were so many things in her life that desperately needed to change, but she couldn't seem to manage any of them.

Then something wonderful happened. She told me, "I was praying but—I wasn't really asking for anything. I just told the Lord I couldn't do *anything* to change myself. But somehow—He answered the cry of my heart. He filled up the empty place in me where 'self' had finally given up trying to make a godly woman. I realized my heart's desire had been right, but my Source had been wrong. It was like a paintbrush trying to paint the picture without the Artist...it's impossible. When I turned the tools of creation over to my Creator, He began to put rich color back into my life."

Sandy is now a writer, gifted artist, and most recently became one of our first-grade Sunday school teachers. I asked her recently how things were going. "I felt pretty confident at first," she said. "After all, how hard can it be to teach first-graders? But one Sunday morning, it just wasn't working for me. I'd prepared the lesson and all that, but I just couldn't get it together. I began telling a story, but the kids started fidgeting. I knew I'd lost them. With a desperate heart I cried, *Lord, help me!* Almost immediately, I heard myself telling the story with ease and excitement. The children focused on every word.

"That really taught me something—that help and strength are just a prayer away. The more I acknowledge my weakness to the Lord with a willingness to be used, the sooner He will strengthen me and use me." She said that as she and the children were leaving the classroom that morning, she heard that sweet, still, small voice of the Lord saying, *I want you to be a voice for Me, but always remember: you're the vessel, I am the Word, and the Holy Spirit is the Teacher.*

Like my friend, Sandy, when I'm called upon to do the unthinkable or the unbelievable, and I try myself, I fail. But when I call on Him, He is always able to handle the situation. When Jesus said to the disciples, "You must forgive people as much as seventy times seven," what was their response? Without hesitation they said, "Lord, then You'd better increase our faith...*real fast.*"

The reason God's call upon our lives seems bigger than we are is because it is. The responsibility of our children, family, work, ministry, and spiritual lives seems bigger than we are because it is. We're not built to live life without God's help; none of us. One of the Good Things about Bad Things is that I discover there are some tasks I just can't do and some situations I simply can't manage; only He can!

I'll never forget staying for a week with a good friend when we were in Bible college. He lived on a farm in Northern California, and every morning his mom would cook up an incredible ranch-style breakfast. Hotcakes and fresh eggs and biscuits and piles of sweet smoky bacon.

Every morning after breakfast, however, his mom would carefully stack the dishes and then disappear for an hour or so. When she came back, her eyes would be red and puffy.

My friend told me this had gone on for years. When he was little, he would ask his mom where she went every day after breakfast. She would always answer, "You wouldn't understand now, son. You're too young."

Finally, when he was a teenager, she told him what he somehow already knew.

"I just go down by the creek, sit under a cotton-wood tree by myself and talk to the Lord," she said. "Every day I tell Him, 'There's no way in a million years I can be the kind of wife you want me to be. There's no chance in a million worlds I can be the kind of mom you want me to be...unless, dear Lord, You help me.'"

Every morning of the world this woman would sit before the Lord by the little stream, lean her back against the rugged bark of the cottonwood and weep out her insufficiency. And every morning of the world He would meet her and provide for her need.

My friend went on to be a pastor. A good one. But he has this strange habit. Every morning, just a little after breakfast, he disappears for an hour or so. And comes back with red, puffy eyes. And down in his secret place, every morning of the world, he weeps before the Lord and tells him, "Lord, there is no way in a million years I can be the kind of husband and dad and pastor You want me to be. I can't begin to do it...unless You do it for me and through me."

My friend eventually told me how this family tradition started. His mother said she read about it in an old book, George M. Truett's *A Quest for Souls.*

Twenty-four years ago, I obtained a copy of that book. It has been a priceless treasure to me ever since. Because of my own obvious limitations, I have chosen to embrace the same tradition. And so every morning I do a similar thing. I don't go and sit down by a cottonwood or running stream. But I do get down on my knees by the old couch in my office and ask the Lord to help me be the kind of husband and dad and pastor He wants me to be.

It's true you know. You can't be the kind of dad or mom God wants you to be until you realize *you can't be one.* Then you can be one.

You can't be the man of God or woman of God you long to be until you realize *you never will be.* Then you'll be closer than ever before.

I remember sitting at my desk in my office eleven years ago. The pressure of a growing church, crushing responsibilities, and exploding opportunities sent me crawling on my knees behind my couch. It was like suddenly waking up in the pilot's seat of a crowded 747 at 30,000 feet with my hands on the controls and realizing *I don't know how to fly this thing. I don't have the slightest idea what to do next. If someone in the control tower doesn't take over and tell me every move to make, I'm going to crash and burn.*

I wanted to hide. I told the Lord, *It's too much. It's too big. It's too important. What You've called me to do and be is bigger than I'll ever be. It's more than I'll ever be capable of doing.*

And He said, "That's right, son."

To be humbled really means to be humiliated. People who are truly humble before God are often *humiliated* while trying to perform the task to which they've been called. They're embarrassed to even admit to trying. They realize that God will have to basically underwrite the whole thing or it will never be done. Period.

People get into trouble when they try to be more, do more, and have more than God has designed. They flippantly quote Philippians 4:13, "I can do all things through Christ who strengthens me." It's a great truth, but so often misapplied. Some believe it to mean you can do anything you want to do, be anything you want to be, go anywhere you want to go. I don't believe that's what Paul is saying. I think he's saying that with the help and strength of Jesus Christ I'll go where He wants me to go, be what He wants me to be, and do what He wants me to do. I once heard my mentor, Jack Hayford, say, "Without Him, we cannot. Without us, He will not."

Thank the Lord it's not size or experience or gifts or talents that make the difference in our lives. It's recognizing our human limitations. We don't like to admit it, but it's true.

We are limited in power; God is not.

We know some things; God knows everything.

We can do a lot of things; God can do anything.

You can't be saved until you know you're lost. You won't be strong until you know you're weak. You won't be faithful until you see you're faithless. You won't be pure until you understand how debased and degraded you are in your own flesh.

Realizing our limitations is grounds for breakthrough. We are limited in intellect. We are limited in performance. We are limited in finance. We are limited in wisdom, power, and love. And that is where our Lord comes in. That is where the plain water becomes fine wine at His creative, compassionate touch.

Not only does He have the power to deal with our limitations, but He can identify with them as well, because He has had personal experience with them. Why did He come to earth in human form? So He could live and work among us, know our limitations and hurts, see the weakness of man's flesh, feel the agony and pain of suffering and death, and yet all the while provide for us access to the unlimited, unparalleled, unfathomable riches of God through His sacrificial death on the cross.

As it says in the book of Hebrews:

Inasmuch then as the children have partaken of flesh and blood, He Himself likewise shared in the same, that through death He might destroy him who had the power of death, that is, the devil, and release those who through fear of death were all their lifetime subject to bondage (Hebrews 2:14-15).

Imagine God, the Creator of the universe, being limited to the constraints of a human body. What humility! Don't let the familiarity of the Sunday school stories blind you to the most astounding reality in history.

It was *God* in that manger.

It was *God* working in that carpenter shop.

It was *God* on that cross.

He had a body, a job, and even grew up in a family just as we do. The Lord also came to earth to explode all of the myths that man has about limitations. The world says: Limitations are a sign of weakness. Limitations cause depression. Limitations signal failure. Limitations are of no value. Limitations are a handicap.

Society says admitting our limitations is a sign of weakness. But Jesus didn't seem to mind announcing to everyone His reliance upon God. He prayed every day, showing His utter dependence upon God. He waited on God's timing, showing His patient obedience to follow God's plan.

Once we are willing to accept our own limits, we must learn how to deal with them. Here are seven practical ways to address the limits in our lives:

1. Recognize them. Circumstances often divide our lives into two parts: that which is manageable and that which is unmanageable. More specifically, circumstances show me what I can do, what God can do, and what we can do together. Knowing the difference makes all the difference.

2. Don't be proud. To postpone asking means to postpone receiving. If I were drowning, I would yell for help. Wouldn't you? Remember that it's possible we won't find the help we need from the Lord if we don't ask.

3. Deal with discouragement. Even when it seems that God's not going to come through, don't worry; He will. We can learn a lesson from Mary. When asked to help at the wedding in Cana, Jesus said, "My hour has not yet come." Then Mary said an interesting thing: "Get ready to do whatever He says." She *knew* the Lord, and she knew from her experience of living with Him that He would not stand by and fail to help someone in need who had humbly asked.

4. Follow instructions. The attitude of our hearts is the key to our own deliverance. Only you can determine to let God make it happen. It's rare that God does anything without letting us be a part of it: look at David's sling and the defeat of Goliath, Noah's hammer in building the ark, and Moses' rod and the parting of the Red Sea. At the wedding at Cana, the servants were told to fill the pitchers with water and then wait and watch.

5. Give God the credit. Read Psalm 116 and learn again what it means to bless God for all His blessings. Walking with God begins to build in us a predisposition to praise Him because our lives are filled with so many demonstrations of His unlimited supply.

6. Don't worry. No matter what you need, He probably has it in stock in the warehouse of heaven. If not, no problem. He'll create it for you.

7. Beware of comparison. God has given all of us talents, gifts, and influence, yet there are always those who have more than we do. Heaven will reveal that there is a world of difference between significance and prominence. The world evaluates the success of a life by one's prominence. If you're rich and influential, you're important. But the Lord says that if you're faithful in even the smallest of things, your life has great significance. Don't compare yourself with anyone. You weren't called or gifted to do their job, and they certainly aren't equipped to do yours.

My job still includes weddings. That fact alone guarantees my position on the ragged edge of humiliation and human limitation.

Just last Saturday two ringbearers and a flower girl had a pre-ceremonial party and ate the bread and drank the juice. That wasn't the problem. The real problem was that I didn't notice it until the bride was coming down the aisle. What did I do? You probably think God loves me so much that He quietly filled the empty glass with juice. He didn't. But what He did do was to cover the situation with grace and gentle humor. Someday I'll tell you about it. It's a great story.

Acknowledging the Bad Thing of limitations is the beginning of many Good Things. In order to move in strength we must acknowledge our weakness. To know our weakness, we must allow the Holy Spirit to scan our soul with the heavenly microscope that probes every nook and cranny in our spiritual lives, searching for anything of self-sufficiency or pride.

He knows just what to do with pride.

CHAPTER SIX

Failure

Having arrested Him, they led Him and brought Him into the high priest's house. But Peter followed at a distance. Now when they had kindled a fire in the midst of the courtyard and sat down together, Peter sat among them. And a certain servant girl, seeing him as he sat by the fire, looked intently at him and said, "This man was also with Him." But he denied Him, saying "Woman, I do not know Him." And after a little while another saw him and said, "You also are of them." But Peter said, "Man, I am not!" Then after about an hour had passed, another confidently affirmed, saying, "Surely this fellow also was with Him, for he is a Galilean." But Peter said, "Man, I do not know what you are saying!" Immediately, while he was still speaking, the rooster crowed. And the Lord turned and looked at Peter. Then Peter remembered the word of the Lord, how He had said to him, "Before the rooster crows, you will deny Me three times." So Peter went out and wept bitterly (Luke 22:54-62).

You haven't watched Monday Night Football until you watch it with a former pro. Talk about color commentary! Who needs instant replay when you're in the same room with a guy who knows all the inside moves?

Steve Thompson, ex-defensive end for the New York Jets, is a good friend of mine. After his retirement, Steve came to live in Portland, and we made Monday night in front of his tube a weekly ritual.

We were both big eaters and both too lazy to get up at half time and go buy the pizza and pop. So we concocted a game to determine who would have to buy. Just before kickoff, we both tried to guess what the half time score would be. The closest one was the winner. The loser would then have to get the refreshments. To make it even more interesting, the guy who came up on the short end would also have to *serve* the winner his pepperoni special.

That was the worst part. Neither of us competitive, "macho" types wanted to be caught serving food to some smirky, demanding guy watching half time highlights in his stocking feet.

But I put a move on Steve Thompson. That former Jet was outflanked and he didn't even know it. What my friend didn't realize was that Monday night games broadcast in Portland were always on a one-hour tape delay. So every week, on the way over to his house, I would listen to the first half of the game—live—on the radio… which increased my chances of success rather significantly.

During one game, on a critical third-and-seven play, Steve turned to me and said, "Okay, hotshot, whaddya think they'll do in this situation?"

I looked at him. "Well, I'm not a sports brain like you, but in my mind there's no question. Number thirty-two will run the ball around the right end."

The big man, with all his years of football knowledge, laughed out loud.

"Don't be ridiculous! This is an obvious passing situation." But sure enough, they ran around the right end. Steve couldn't believe it. For the rest of the evening he kept looking at me out of the corner of his eye.

On another occasion my team was facing a forty-eight-yard field goal attempt.

"Well Reverend, do you think he'll put it through?"

"Hmmm. I dunno Steve. You're the pro. But from where I sit this guy looks a little shaky. I think he'll make it, but…I think it'll bounce off the ummm…left upright before it goes through."

The announcer interrupted me. *"It looks long enough—but a little off center. It's going…CAN YOU BELIEVE IT? Whoa! It hit the left upright and went in! Who could have called that?"*

"You want Canadian bacon and pineapple or pepperoni?" Steve asked.

This went on for *weeks*. After a while, my big buddy was feeling like a real failure. Over the course of many Mondays, Steve became convinced I was either a consummate sports genius or consistently moved with the spiritual gift of knowledge. I was tempted to try and work my plan for the whole season. After all, I was the struggling young pastor of a small church, had no NFL pension, and good pizza is expensive. But wouldn't you know it, I had an attack of conscience. I finally confessed. Over the phone, I might add. He's six foot six, and you can never be too careful.

Wouldn't it be nice to know the endings of certain things before you ever begin? (Just think of all the pizza and root beer you could rack up.) In some situations, of course, you *can* know the ending. Such as listening to the radio before you watch it on TV. Such as reading the book before you see the movie. Such as peeking at the last page before you start chapter 1. Such as stacking the deck before you play Old Maid. But most of the time, you and I have no clue how events will work themselves out in our lives.

Just for a moment, imagine we could peek ahead through the years and see how certain things in our lives were going to wrap up. Could we then come back to the present time and manipulate situations and events to achieve greater "success"?

I'm not sure we could. I'm not at all confident you and I understand what success really means.

Most of us tend to determine victory and success by the scoreboard. We define success as prosperity, power, prestige, points—or maybe free pizza. As long as that's what we're after, that's often what we'll get. All those things are wonderful and good.

But...

Have you ever realized a dream and then, after possessing it, wondered what all the shouting was about? You finally build that new house and furnish it with all the latest gadgets. You finally land that promotion, woo that girl of your dreams, walk away with the college diploma, buy the new sectional couch, or pocket the keys for that new, red Toyota four-by-four. But inside, there's still that empty feeling—like the line in that old Peggy Lee song, *"Is that all, is that all there is?"*

Could it be that our personal definition of success is over-rated? Could the Bad Thing we call "failure" actually be a Good Thing—or *part* of a Good Thing—in disguise?

I counsel people from time to time who are outwardly successful, but inwardly miserable failures. Not by my definition, but *theirs.* They may be attractive, well-dressed, and financially prosperous, but in every other area of life they're utterly bankrupt and desolate. With all the best intentions, they drove their silver BMW 325i straight into a black, bottomless marsh.

Good intentions can only go so far and do so much.

Peter, the disciple, had laudable intentions. He was committed and devoted to Christ. He would eventually be considered the Lord's spokesman and leader of the Twelve. Yet, let's face it. His score card was scary reading. His field goals sailed consistently wide of the mark—or never got off the ground. Any coach but Jesus Christ would have sent him to the showers with a one-way ticket home.

In Galilee, he tried to walk on water—and then the sea bottom.

In the Upper Room, he said Jesus would never wash

his feet—and then promptly asked for a bath.

In the hour of his Master's greatest emotional trial—he slept like a guy in a mattress commercial.

At the arrest in the garden, he flailed about with a sword, delivered a mortal blow to a slave's right ear—and then ran for his life.

Peter didn't want to fail, but he did. Nobody wants to fail. But everybody does. I've never met anyone who deliberately set out to mess up his or her life. I've performed a lot of weddings, but I've never heard anyone say at a ceremony, "Over the next few months, we plan to trash this relationship." I've done a lot of baby dedications, but I've never heard a mom or dad say, "We plan on neglecting this child, or spoiling this child, or for sure alienating this child before she reaches her teens." Most of us are counting on a smooth, freeway ride through life with no speed traps.

But there are traps.

And they sometimes appear where you'd least expect them.

I want you to consider three common failure traps. But hang on...they're not the ones you might expect.

Trap #1: Knowledge

How many times have I heard, "What this country needs is more education. Education will lift us out of poverty and crime and despair. Education is the golden key to success and happiness." And how many times have I heard people quote Christ's words, "Know the truth and the truth will make you free"? Jesus did say that. And it is true. But knowledge alone has never kept anyone from failing at anything! Look at Peter. Imagine all he learned sitting for three years under the profound teaching ministry of the Nazarene, and observing the miraculous ministry that flowed from His life. He heard and saw things that were the heart's desire of ancient kings and prophets.

Let's look at it another way. For three years of your life, you walk, talk, eat, sleep, and take long walking tours with *God Himself* as your constant companion and tutor. You have a three-year lease with the Creator of the Universe as your roommate.

In addition to that, Peter *knew* that he would deny the Lord. He knew that terrible failure loomed just around the bend. He knew what was coming, because Jesus told him so.

> Peter answered and said to Him, "Even if all are made to stumble because of You, I will never be made to stumble." Jesus said to him, "Assuredly, I say to you that this night, before the rooster crows, you will deny Me three times" (Matthew 26:33-34).

But on that excruciating night of denial, all that Peter had learned and heard and experienced was not enough to keep him from failing his dearest Friend.

You can't depend on knowledge to keep you from failing. It won't.

Trap #2: Revelation

It was Peter who declared, "You are the Christ, the Son of the living God." It was a Mount Everest moment. The grandstands of heaven must have exploded. The Son of God Himself affirmed that Peter was speaking the very words of the Father. In our vernacular, Jesus said, "Peter, you did not figure this out all by yourself. You may be bright, but you're not *that* bright. What you've just said is not a matter of adding two plus two and coming up with four. You've experienced a moment of revelation and you are a blessed man because of it!"

Pretty heady stuff. One-and-a-half minutes later, however, the Lord was sternly rebuking Peter for becoming a mouthpiece for Satan. Revelation didn't keep Peter from failure. Nor has it kept anyone else from failing. It never will. It's not supposed to.

Think of Adam and Eve. Think of twilight walks along fragrant garden paths with Almighty God. And think how far they fell.

Think of Solomon, the wisest human being on the planet—ever. And think how he died like a common fool.

Think of the Corinthians—"rich," "kingly," "wise," "strong," and "lacking in no spiritual gifts." And think how they tolerated unbelievable sin in their midst and fought among themselves like a bunch of kids in a schoolyard.

Some of the saddest moments of my pastoring life have happened as I've sat with people who have "seen the things of God" like few others, yet were bewildered by the failure of their marriage, or their personal sin.

Don't depend on revelation to keep you from failing. It won't.

Trap #3: Love

I have wept with many who have confessed a passionate love for Jesus, yet have blundered into deep canyons of moral failure. I don't think anyone loved Jesus more than Peter. But not even love kept Peter from shouting, "I don't know the Man!" So often, anguished, stumbling saints find themselves thinking, "I DO love Him. How could I have done this? *How could I have failed Him?*" The next logical step is, "I must not love Him. If I did, I wouldn't have failed."

That's a lie our culture teaches. Watch a soap opera. Read a novel. Listen to popular music. You'll hear it again and again: "Love is the answer." No, it's not! It's important. It's essential. It's critical. But it's not the answer.

Perhaps the hardest moment of Peter's life was the post-Easter conversation in Galilee:

"Simon, do you love Me?"

"Yes."

Second time: "Simon, do you love Me?"

"Yes."

And again: "Do you love Me?"

Peter's frustration and heart-break finally gushes out like water from a broken levee. "Lord, You know everything. You knew where the 153 fish were we just caught. You knew how You'd feed the multitude. You saw Nathanael while he was dreaming under a fig tree. You *know* what's in my heart. You know that I love You. You know that I denied You. I don't understand how I can both love You and deny You but, yes, I do love You."

In Peter's world, too, the popular thought was, "If you loved me, you wouldn't do that." It didn't work then. It won't work now.

Don't depend on love to keep you from failing or falling. It won't.

Knowledgeable people fail everyday; they just do it

with more class. People blessed by revelation fail, too; their fall just sounds louder. And people in love with Jesus fail as well; their pain and agony are just a little more profound.

In the emotional rubble left from his betrayal, Peter was far from ready to be the keynote speaker on the Day of Pentecost, and far from ready for the role of martyr that he would ultimately assume.

But he was on his way.

The bewildered apostle may not have realized it at the time, but he was on a journey. Peter had no knowledge of his final destination, so how could he identify landmarks along the way? Only Jesus knew what lay ahead.

Our Lord loves taking people who have been buried by failure and digging them out. Perhaps, as Jesus looked at Peter in that courtyard, His compassionate eyes were saying, *Peter, I know you're trying, and I know you truly do love Me. You don't know it now, dear friend, but one day you will be called to lay down your life for Me...and you will. You won't run. You won't hide. You won't deny. You will boldly stand, and in the face of death and blood and torture and humiliation, you will own Me as Lord and Christ.*

Jesus knew Peter's denial was not the end but a beginning. He knew that people often fail along life's journey before they succeed.

I was raised in the Midwest. Back there (and back then) it was a big deal to go for a "drive" on Sunday afternoon. The destination didn't matter much, if there even was one. Mom and Dad said that just being together was what was important. We might wind up going to

Dairy Queen, visiting relatives, or buying some cider at the country store. Sometimes I loved those trips, and sometimes I hated them. We'd all climb into the old Chevy and roll on down the road, kind of like the Waltons or the Beverly Hillbillies (or, in our case, the "Bloomington Bunch"—Bloomington, Minnesota, that is). Sometimes we'd sing a song or play a game such as counting cows, looking for out-of-state license plates, or scanning the landscape for anything with the color red in it.

Those trips became great memories for me. Success in the Christian life is like that. It's a memorable journey, not a destination. Yes, we get flat tires sometimes, but that doesn't mean we're stalled forever. Yes, we get lost sometimes, but that doesn't mean we'll never make it home.

For Peter, the journey that led to dependence passed by two significant milestones: *confession* and *repentance*.

Confession

Before Peter could know the joys of living in victory, he had to admit defeat. He had to acknowledge failure. He had to confess the error of his way. Confession is the first step in our journey back because it brings us to the place we belong.

Failure moves us out of position, sin moves us away from the presence and glory of God, away from receiving from His hand what we need to succeed. I once found a quote written on the overleaf of my mom's Bible. I don't know who the author was, but the words have marked my life.

Sin will take you farther than you want to go.
Sin will keep you longer than you want to stay.
Sin will cost you more than you want to pay.

For most of us, the word "confession" brings to

mind, "If we confess our sins, He is faithful and just to forgive us our sins and to cleanse us from all unrighteousness" (1 John 1:9). I love that verse. But I'm thinking of the word confession as a *declaration*. Before we can hope to get on with our lives or help someone else, some important confessions need to be made.

First, we confess to the Lord, "I love You." We would rather say we're sorry. It's easier for us to say, "Trust me, Lord, it'll never happen again." But we can learn an important lesson in Peter's conversation with the Lord in John 21.

The Lord wasn't as interested in Peter's confession of guilt as He was in Peter's confession of love and realization of need. Jesus said, "Simon, son of Jonah, do you love Me?" He didn't say, "Simon, are you failure-free?" or, "Simon, are you *really* sorry?" or, "Simon, will you swear right now never to fail Me again?"

But the wisdom of God brings an honest man, a sincere man, one who has failed in his attempt to keep his promise, to something even more painful than the whipping post. For us, like for Peter, it is far more painful and difficult to declare our love and need for the Savior in the face of having so horribly failed Him.

Second, we should confess to the Lord what we believe about ourselves and Satan: "I have no righteousness of my own. I am only righteous by the blood of Jesus Christ." Or maybe, after reading again Romans 6 through 8, we might declare, "I am NOT a slave of sin, I am a slave of righteousness. I am NOT under the power of sin, I have been set free. I am NOT a prisoner of my flesh, I can walk every day in the power of the Spirit and in newness of life."

I've heard it explained this way: the enemy is like a bacteria. Bacteria has no power to wound but, if you get wounded, bacteria has the opportunity to bring about infection.

Failure is beyond the power of the enemy. He can assist it, he can attempt to make it happen; he cannot force it. Failure is a product of human effort (see James 1:13-16). Hell will help all it can, but in the final analysis, failure is our responsibility, not Satan's.

When failure occurs, I first tell the Lord I'm His. Then I tell the enemy I'm not his! Satan has access to my life only when I complicate my failure by refusing to acknowledge it, or when I attempt to "fix things" in my own strength.

Repentance

Repentance is a decision to go another way, to trust the Lord rather than yourself, to admit His way is the right way. The best way to start your journey back to blessing and success is to stop. Stop trying to do it all on your own. Stop making promises to God and to yourself unless you've made a serious decision to rely upon God's power and grace to get it done.

The Good Thing about the Bad Thing of Peter's early wrong turns is that they eventually led him to *right* turns. Not only that, he was able in his later years to draw a road map for young Christians so that *they* might avoid wrong turns and dead-ends.

In 1 Peter 4:7 he wrote, "Therefore be serious and watchful in your prayers." *Could he have been remembering the time in the garden when he fell asleep?*

In 1 Peter 3:8-9, he penned, "Be tenderhearted, be

courteous; not returning evil for evil or reviling for revil-ing, but on the contrary blessing." *Could he have been remembering his own lamentable surgery on Malchus's right ear?*

In 1 Peter 3:15, he urged, "Always be ready to give a defense to everyone who asks you a reason for the hope that is in you." *Could he have been recalling a young maid's pointed question one cold dawn by a charcoal fire?*

In 1 Peter 1:5, he told believers, "[We] are kept by the power of God through faith." *Could he have been thinking back to a black night on a stormy sea when he felt himself sinking and—powerless to rescue himself—cried out his fear and despair to the Lord Jesus? Might he have been remembering that strong Carpenter's hand that pulled him out of the sea and led him through the storm?*

The Good Thing about the Bad Thing of Peter's fail-ures is what he learned through it all: he learned that drastic, radical dependence on Christ was his only hope for success. As someone told me early in my ministry, "God is not obligated to help anyone who isn't totally dependent upon Him."

I remember hearing a pastor friend of mine, Stan Simmons, tell about an experience he had on one of those Saturday all-church work days. Stan went down-stairs and came around the corner only to find a little boy turning the light switch off and on, off and on. Stan said, "Son, don't do that." The little boy reluctantly stopped and waddled off to find other more important jobs to do.

Moments later, Stan and one of the men were attempting to carry a large, collapsible table upstairs, when the little boy reappeared, making it clear he wanted to help. So here was this two-foot-tall child trying to "help" carry a heavy wooden table up a narrow church stairway. Actually, he was having some trouble getting up the stairs by himself, and ended up leaning on the table more than lifting it.

Once the trio reached the top of the stairs, the boy wanted to quickly set the legs down, but forgot to lock them in place. Just at the right moment, the boy's dad stepped in behind him and secured each one.

Then came the finale. Stan and the boy's father were talking and glanced over to see that the little guy had climbed on top of the table and there, standing alone, had lifted both arms above his head like Rocky winning the world heavy-weight championship. He proudly flexed his little biceps as if he had carried, set up, and secured the table all by himself.

"At that moment," Stan told me, "I heard the Lord say, *That's the way you are with Me sometimes. I carry the tables, set them up, and secure them. Then I let you stand on top and look good.*"

Go ahead and try to carry your own table. Try to succeed on your own. It won't work. The Christian life can't be lived without the life of Christ. If you depend upon yourself, you probably won't be depending upon Him. If you depend upon your knowledge, your profound spiritual experiences, or your deep love for the Lord Jesus, your family, or your fellow man, you won't be depending upon Him. Living *in* Him is the way to live *for* Him. Depending upon Him is what makes you dependable.

Thankfully, our Lord has made it easy for us to depend upon Him: He is always available. He is always close by. As certainly as He accompanied Peter on his journey from failure to success, so He will walk with us. He has given us the gift of the Holy Spirit, the One who takes His place "at my side."

If I want to make the journey from failure to success, the critical issue is *dependence*...upon Jesus and Jesus alone. The wonderful thing about knowing Jesus, about being His friend, is that He knows that failure can lead to success. He, and He alone, knows the beginning from the end.

Do you find yourself at half time in your life facing a lopsided score, a crushed spirit, muffed opportunities, and a host of cynics who are more than ready to write off your chances?

Now's no time to listen to the crowds, check the box score, or talk to the media. The only voice you need to hear is that of your Coach. He has the plan for turning your failures into unbelievable scoring opportunities. If He tells you to stop fretting and put your trust in Him, you'd better do it.

He's the only one who knows how the game will end. And He doesn't even need a radio.

CHAPTER SEVEN

Loneliness

Very early in the morning, while it was still dark, Jesus got up, left the house and went off to a solitary place, where he prayed....

Jesus answered them, "Do you now believe? Indeed the hour is coming, yes, has now come, that you will be scattered, each to his own, and will leave Me alone. And yet I am not alone, because the Father is with Me" (Mark 1:35, NIV; John 16:31-32).

The sign on the bus read "Niobrara or Bust"—as in Niobrara, Nebraska.

We were crawling along Minnesota State Highway

35 in our used-up, faded-blue church bus. This was the same bus that towed snow-bound cars out of the parking lot during winter and hauled sod for the church's new yard in the spring. We kids called it "the Lord's Limo," because it shuttled our youth group to outings, Youth for Christ rallies, and, in this case, junior high camp.

Our vintage chariot was coughing and doddering its way toward Nebraska loaded with sleeping bags, suitcases, radios, musical instruments, and the compressed clamor of seventeen excited teenagers.

Junior high camp, of course, meant that for the first time hormones were kicking into gear. When hormones mix with a long bus ride, a natural phenomenon occurs. Teenagers begin to stick together. Like magnets, they attract. Jane clings to Bill, Carl sticks with Carol, and so on.

On every bus load, however, it seems like there's an uneven number. It wasn't long before I discovered I was odd man out. There were pairs and spares, and I was a spare. A leftover.

I sat in my cold, hard seat, feeling like the rapture had taken place and I was the only one left on the planet, or I had the bubonic plague, or something. I'd never felt so lonely.

But then there was Bubba. He was the youth pastor's dog, a mutt who traveled with us everywhere we went. I remember sitting alone, feeling sorry for myself, and then suddenly there was ol' Bubba in the seat beside me, looking at me with inquiring eyes. It wasn't long before he was snorting and licking my face like an all-day sucker. That made me feel a little better.

"At least," I told myself, "*someone* loves me."

It wasn't until later I learned that dogs like salt. And

with the combination of tears and sweat, my face made for a blue-plate special.

You've heard it said that you can be loneliest in the middle of a crowd. That's really true. Maybe you were the boy chosen last in a game of sandlot football. Maybe you were the girl no one asked to the prom. Maybe you can remember being left standing alone because the person you were with chose someone else. That's how I felt on that bus ride. And when you're an adolescent, you can take any adult emotion you care to choose and intensify it by a factor of ten. Most teens don't have any kind of emotional calluses or padding. All those delicate self-image nerves are right there on the surface, and the hurt goes bone deep.

When I got home, I told Mom what happened. "I'll *never* go with that stupid, cliquish, arrogant bunch of bums again," I fumed. "I'll never ride that dumb bus again."

Mom was all diplomacy. "Son," she said, "all those girls were probably thinking, 'He's too good for me. He's too handsome for me,' so they went for a lesser guy. Besides, son, if you're ever feeling lonely, remember I love you."

Right at that moment those words weren't very comforting. They *pay* moms to say stuff like that. It's nice, but that's kind of like being kissed by your sister or coming in first in a one-man race. It just doesn't zing.

We all face times of feeling abandoned and lonely. Counselors tell us that the number one problem plaguing people today isn't fear, insecurity, or rejection. It's loneliness. Isolation. Longing for companionship. I was talking with a woman recently who said, with pain in her eyes, "I've been lonely since I was a little girl. Ever since I can remember, I've felt isolated and alone."

In Psalm 22, David penned what so many of us

have felt: *"My God, my God, why have you forsaken me?
Why do you refuse to help me or even listen to my
groans?" (Psalm 22:1, TLB).*

So what's the Good Thing about the Bad Thing of
loneliness? What could be good about feeling like your
only friend is Bubba, and even he has ulterior motives?

David's message in Psalm 27 contains a perfect kernel
of wisdom, "When I'm alone," he says, "and my enemies
have come to destroy me, though I'm outnumbered and
even my parents have forsaken me, I will wait on the Lord."

You and I aren't the first ones to wrestle with feelings of loneliness. David did. And he learned something
during those times. As the years have gone by, I've been
learning something, too. I've begun to realize that God,
my Father, may have had a hand in *arranging* those
lonely seasons, with a good purpose in mind.

When I was dating Joyce, I did all kinds of bizarre
things to be with her. I had surveillance on her the
moment she stepped onto campus. I memorized her
daily schedule. I knew when she came home from work.
When she ate breakfast. What door she'd come out of in
the morning.

I'd plan times during the day to intersect her life just
so I could be near her. When she went to the library at
9:05 A.M., I'd be there. When she ate at 5:15 P.M. in the
dorm, I'd be there.

I felt the call to attend her church, and even joined
the street ministry team that she was a part of.

She couldn't believe the coincidences in our sched-
ules. She couldn't believe our interests were so similar
and that we always ran into each other.

I could. I planned it.

I went to incredible lengths to calculate and design those "chance" encounters with this young woman I was growing to love so much. Is it really such a stretch to believe that God, in His love, might watch our daily routine and then from time to time arrange a private encounter with you and me?

It often seems that those priceless meetings are preceded by a period of loneliness and pain. I'm reminded of the venerable prophet Elijah, who, after confronting a conspiracy of desperate evil in his country and its rulers, fled to the wilderness and lapsed into deep, almost suicidal depression. After forty days of utter isolation, he crawled into a mountain cave and spent the night. Sometime in the middle of the night, the Lord arranged a little demonstration for His despondent servant.

> Then [the LORD] said, "Go out and stand on the mountain before the LORD." And behold, the LORD passed by, and a great and strong wind tore into the mountains and broke the rocks in pieces before the LORD, but the LORD was not in the wind; and after the wind an earthquake, but the LORD was not in the earthquake; and after the earthquake a fire, but the LORD was not in the fire; and after the fire a still small voice. So it was, when Elijah heard it, that he wrapped his face in his mantle and went out and stood in the entrance of the cave. Suddenly a voice came to him, and said, "What are you doing here, Elijah?" (1 Kings 19:11-13).

I'm both moved and disturbed by this passage. How often, in the backwash of turbulent emotions and stormy circumstances have I failed to listen for that "still, small voice"? Elijah heard the merest of whispers, and instinctively recognized the voice of his God. Crawling out of his cave that starry night, he received new instructions—and a big dose of fresh encouragement. That encouragement included a road map to a new friend and companion to share the prophet's load...a young man named Elisha.

But a whisper is soft, while pain shouts loud and long...he could have so easily missed God's gentle comfort.

Sometimes we do.

A friend of mine recently reflected back on a critical year during his college days. At the beginning of his junior year, he received a "Dear John" letter from a long-time girlfriend attending school in another part of the country. That disappointing letter coincided with his planned launch of a new ministry with the youth in a local church. He described how the breakup first sent him into sullen depression, then launched him into a frantic series of shallow, unhappy dating relationships—one after another—virtually ruining any opportunity for ministry that year.

"I wonder now if the Lord wanted to communicate something special to me in that transitional year," my friend mused. "I wonder if He wanted me to take a new step in my walk with Him. I'll never know. Instead of listening for His voice, I became so desperate in my loneliness I started chasing girl after girl. I went backward that year."

My friend was suggesting that God may have arranged that period of loneliness in his life to speak to him in a deeper way than he had ever experienced. But he was so enmeshed in a self-centered turmoil he refused to listen—and perhaps missed a priceless opportunity.

It *is* difficult to listen for God's voice in those excruciating moments of lonely isolation. But in every instance when I have genuinely chosen to seek Him in such a season, I have been amply rewarded.

I remember so well my freshman year of Bible college in Los Angeles. One of my classes that year was Homiletics—where they teach you how to preach. One of our assignments was to prepare a sermon, deliver it in front of the entire class, and then listen as the class critiqued it. I was a young, bashful Midwestern boy, and the thought of standing in front of an indifferent, critical audience like that turned my insides into jelly.

As it turned out, I had every reason to be apprehensive. My sermon was horrible. An unqualified disaster. The delivery was bad. The structure was bad. The illustrations were bad. It was just plain bad. Halfway through I wanted to put a paper bag over my head.

When I finally lurched to a finish, the stone-faced professor turned in his big squeaky chair and faced my classmates.

"Okay," he said. "Tell me what you liked about Ron's sermon." Dead quiet. Not a hand was raised.

"Was there anything that moved you?" No hands. Nothing.

"Was there anything that convicted your heart?" Utter silence. I could hear the pounding of my own heart.

He pursed his lips and pressed his fingertips together. "Well," he said quietly, "was there anything that *bothered* you? What problems do you foresee for Ron? Where do you think he could improve? What could he do better?"

That took the cork off the bottle. A forest of hands shot up.

I felt like a lonely piece of meat in a bowl filled

with piranha. When they finished chewing on me, it was all I could do to keep from crying.

I walked out of class, stumbled across campus, slipped into the quiet darkness of the college prayer room, and dropped to my knees. I felt sick to my stomach, deeply hurt, and so, so alone.

"Lord," I whispered into the darkness, "You know I want to be a pastor. You know I want to be a preacher, but—I guess I can't preach."

Then, all alone, I heard His voice in my heart as clearly as I've ever heard it before.

You did good, son. You did your best. You don't need to BE the best. I am pleased with you.

It was during that time alone with the Lord that I realized it was Him I needed to please. It was Him I wanted to honor. During that time alone, I discovered the Lord working something of great value in me. My hunger for ministry grew rather than faded.

In God's mind, it seems there are some things that can only be accomplished when we're alone with Him.

God arranged for Jacob to be alone that fearful night by the fords of the Jabbok. With Jacob however, God had something more in mind than a fireside chat. They wrestled violently through the long dark hours. At daybreak, Jacob received a new identity, a promise of blessing, and a permanent reminder of his dependence.

Young Joseph must have felt unspeakably lonely in his Egyptian prison cell, so far from home, jailed on a trumped-up charge by a bored and lecherous nobleman's wife. But it was in that period of enforced solitude that God taught him how to interpret dreams. When the opportune call came from Pharaoh, the only thing Joseph lacked was a shower and a shave.

How empty and desolate Jeremiah must have felt as he sat on the hillside and looked out over the smoking ruins of Jerusalem. Thousands of his countrymen had been slaughtered by the merciless Babylonian invaders. Thousands more had been marched over the horizon in chains. "How lonely sits the city that was full of people," the grieving prophet wrote. Yet in the midst of his agony, he made the discovery of a lifetime—a truth so sustaining that *millions* have dined on it down through the millennia:

> This I recall to my mind,
> Therefore I have hope.
> Through the LORD's mercies we are not consumed,
> Because His compassions fail not.
> They are new every morning;
> Great is Your faithfulness.
> "The LORD is my portion," says my soul,
> "Therefore I hope in Him!"
>
> The LORD is good to those who wait for Him,
> To the soul who seeks Him.
> It is good that one should hope and wait quietly
> For the salvation of the LORD
> (Lamentations 3:21-26).

Even the Son of God faced times when He felt abandoned and alone. Peering ahead through the centuries, the prophet could feel the ache of this young Man's loneliness. "He is despised and rejected by men," Isaiah wrote. "A Man of sorrows and acquainted with grief. And we hid, as it were our faces from Him; He was despised, and we did not esteem Him" (Isaiah 53:3). At the most crucial moment, His closest friends scattered like leaves on a windy night, and left Him alone with His enemies. At the cross He was surrounded by a crowd, but hung alone between earth and heaven. Earth had rejected Him. Heaven saw Him covered with our sins and turned its back. When He realized He had been abandoned by His heavenly Father, He cried out the words of His human father David, "My God, My God, why have You forsaken me?" (Mark 15:34).

And do you know what was good about that worst of all moments in history? Because of what the Lord Jesus endured in those black hours of distilled hell, you and I will never have to be lonely again. Jesus walked alone because only He could travel that Calvary road and only He could go to the cross. He, and He alone, could fulfill all prophecy. Only He, the pure, holy, sinless Son of God, could die for man's sin.

So how can you and I make the Bad Thing of loneliness a Good Thing?

First, realize that our loneliest moments may be arranged by God.

We don't always understand, and even cry out, "Lord, let this cup pass from me!" But there can be ministry in loneliness. There can be value in loneliness. If we submit to those times, God will teach us.

I recently received a letter from Carissa, a precious twelve-year-old girl in our congregation. Just a few months earlier, her family moved to a new neighborhood and she found herself spending many long afternoons by herself. Unlike her parents and us older folk who often cherish solitude, she experienced deep feelings of loneliness. But this insightful, sensitive girl allowed her loneliness to bring her to a wonderful discovery.

She wrote:

One Sunday Pastor Rick preached and one of his points was on loneliness. He said to conquer loneliness you must have purpose. I began to ask myself, *What is my purpose?* and God began to work in my heart. A week or two later Ismael, (a pastor) from Guatemala, spoke on conquering deserts in your life. Then it clicked. God's purpose for my loneliness was to show me my need to spend more time with Him. After that, I began to spend great quantities of time with the Lord, and He began to bless me more than I would ever have imagined.

Pastor, you said once to remember the times you were closest to the Lord and to begin to do what you were practicing then to regain that closeness. The period right after the loneliness experience was a very close time between me and the Lord. I strive to regain that closeness and intimacy.

Carissa had the wisdom and courage to go beneath the empty ache of her unwanted solitude to listen for God's voice. And she was rewarded in a way she will never forget.

Second, decide in advance how you will face those inevitable periods of loneliness and isolation.

I remember when I went on my first date. I had it all planned. I knew what we'd do, where we'd go, and what I'd wear. Don't let that precious time with the Lord be wasted. Let me suggest that you think about what you'll say and how you'll pray and what you'll do beforehand.

Do you have three or four people you need to bring before the Lord in prayer? Do you have several verses you'd like to get down on three-by-five cards to really think about and chew on? Do you have a couple of areas in your life that continually confuse and frustrate you—things you'd like to spread out before your Father for His counsel? Be ready for lonely moments when they come, and if they don't come, get away by yourself and *find* some.

Third, let your loneliness sensitize you to the heartache of others.

We live in a desperately lonely world. Many of us with stable homes and loving church families feel somewhat insulated from the awful emptiness experienced by so many around the world. We sometimes forget that on this cursed, broken planet, loneliness and hopelessness are as common in the atmosphere as oxygen and carbon dioxide. Paul speaks of those who are "without hope, and without God in the world." *That describes the majority of people in your town, in your neighborhood.* Sometimes God allows us a taste of that thirst...just to remind us that we are stewards of a full canteen.

Years ago I was invited to speak in Hong Kong. When services were concluded one afternoon, I felt the desire to wander and be among the Chinese people. To this day I'm not sure how, but somehow I ended up on a little junk way out in the harbor. What space that wasn't filled by crates of pigs and chickens on that odorous little vessel was packed full of Chinese passengers.

Out on the water, something strange began to happen. I began to feel an overwhelming sense of isolation. There I sat on a crate of chickens, feeling increasingly out of place with my white skin, white tennis shoes, and six-foot-four frame. I was alone. I had no idea where I was or where we were going. It was getting dark. I couldn't speak a word of their language and they couldn't speak a word of mine. As the sun slipped lower on the horizon, a sense of panic began to wrap itself around my throat.

Now the Lord reassured me out on that boat, and I eventually found my way back to the hotel. But I will never forget the hollow, barren feeling that washed over me that evening on the South China Sea. It was just a tiny taste of what many in my own city are feeling as I write these words. There is more than one way to feel adrift and alone on a foreign sea. Consider...

> *a mom sitting by a window, waiting for her runaway to come home.*
> *a foreign student on a strange American campus.*
> *a newly-widowed woman in a Bible class full of couples.*
> *a young felon suddenly facing twenty-years-to-life.*
> *a divorced dad unlocking the door of his dark and empty apartment.*
> *a pregnant teenager realizing life can never be the same.*

There is more than enough loneliness to go around. If God has allowed you to experience some of it, remember Paul's words in 2 Corinthians 1:3-4:

> Blessed be the God and Father of our Lord Jesus Christ, the Father of mercies and God of all comfort, who comforts us in all our tribulation, that we may be able to comfort those who are in any trouble, with the comfort with which we ourselves are comforted by God.

Fourth, use those times as a prompt to reach out beyond yourself.

It hardly seems possible that Jesus, in all His torment on the cross, could think of anything but His own suffering. But at the foot of the cross, Christian fellowship was born. In His dying moments, He saw to it that His mother would have a home with John the Beloved. He saw to it that the repentant thief at His side would have a home with Him in heaven.

Sometimes the answer to loneliness is reaching out to someone else, even when we don't feel like it. Sometimes the pain is so deep, we *want* to withdraw. We create our own walls of loneliness because we think no one will understand or care.

But when Jesus saw His mother, for one brief moment He forgot His own cross and remembered hers. When the thief cried, "Lord, remember me when You come into Your kingdom," He knew there was someone far worse off than He. For unless He responded to that cry, the thief must surely die without hope.

Loneliness can be like a silent alarm, reminding you to write that note of encouragement, pick up that phone to call a lonely friend, or walk down the street to visit at a retirement home. I recently heard of a widow in her seventies who spends several days a week in the therapy pool at a children's hospital, helping little ones stretch and exercise their injured bodies. Her apartment is still dark and lonely when she comes home at night, but the fresh memories of smiles and laughter and little reaching hands tend to warm the long evenings.

There isn't the slightest current of loneliness that blows through our hearts that our loving Father doesn't see and understand. Before you turn to frantic activity, empty noise, or blank despair, lift your eyes and see if there is something He might want to say to you in those lonely moments.

He knows your needs and deepest longings. He knows when you need an Elisha who will share your load.

He even knows when you need a Bubba.

110

CHAPTER EIGHT

Hard Choices

Then Jesus came with them to a place called Gethsemane, and said to the disciples, "Sit here while I go and pray over there." And He took with Him Peter and the two sons of Zebedee, and He began to be sorrowful and deeply distressed. Then He said to them, "My soul is exceedingly sorrowful, even to death. Stay here and watch with Me." He went a little farther and fell on His face, and prayed, saying, "O My Father, if it is possible, let this cup pass from Me; nevertheless, not as I will, but as You will." Then He came to the disciples and found them sleeping, and said to Peter, "What? Could you not watch with Me one hour? Watch and pray, lest you enter into temptation. The spirit indeed is willing, but the flesh is weak." Again, a second time, He went away and prayed, saying, "O My Father, if this cup cannot pass away from Me unless I drink it, Your will be done" (Matthew 26:36-42).

In fifty-five years of ministry Brother Eddy had seen it all.

As a young pastor, I had several occasions to spend time with this seasoned Wisconsin minister, now with the Lord. I drank up his advice like a thirsty athlete gulps Gatorade.

We'd been talking about making wise choices, and Brother Eddy paused for a moment, smiled, and then shook his head. Placing a blue-veined hand on my knee, he rasped, "Let me tell you about a woman who came to me once for advice." He went on to relate the account.

The woman was very distraught. She sat in the chair by Brother Eddy's desk, twisting her handkerchief. "Please help me," she said, "I'm very confused."

"Tell me about it," he said.

"Well, you see, I'm married."

"Well," said my friend, a bit bewildered, "you shouldn't be confused about that."

"No, that's not the problem," she replied. "You see, I'm married, but I'm living with another man."

"Ah," sighed Brother Eddy, a knowing look crossing his face. "Well, that certainly would seem grounds for confusion."

She grew more animated. "No, no, you don't

understand. *That's* not the problem. The problem is I'm married to one man, living with another, but I'm in love with a third!"

This wise, gracious pastor looked at her and said in a way only he could, "Honey, you're not confused, *you're stupid!* Now what do you think is the right thing to do in this situation?"

"I guess I should go back to my husband," came the embarrassed reply.

"And what are you *going* to do?"

"I don't know. I'm very confused."

Knowing the right thing to do and actually doing it are different propositions, aren't they? It's one thing to be confused over right and wrong; it's quite another to be confused over what to do about it.

In *The Wizard of Oz,* Scarecrow needed a brain. The Tin Man needed a heart. Dorothy needed a ticket home. And the Lion—oh, yes, the Lion—he needed courage. When I know what to do and don't do it, it's usually because I don't have the courage or the will. Most of us already know what's right. We need the courage to act on what we know.

Sometimes, the situation seems to demand more courage than we can summon. It's a hard choice. An agonizing choice. As a Christian woman who had just left her husband told a friend of mine: "Oh, I *know* what to do. I *know* what the Bible says. I just don't *feel* like doing it. I can't bear to face it."

Throughout our lives, choices constantly test us. To be more accurate, life *is* choice. Every day, every waking hour, we're called upon to make choices about our use of time, our activities, our family, our spouse, our job, our children, our responsibilities, our walk with the Lord. Choosing to obey isn't a one-time event; it's a lifestyle. Sometimes it's easy. Sometimes it's excruciatingly hard. Along the way, many of us have found ourselves wondering, "What's the Good Thing about the Bad Thing of hard choices?"

It's also a fact that many small choices will eventually lead us to big choices. And sometimes those big choices take other choices away from us.

Some time ago I visited with an inmate at the Oregon State Penitentiary. At one crucial point in his life, he chose to attempt an armed robbery. He was apprehended. From that point on, he didn't have to worry about wrestling with an array of decisions.

"When I made *that* choice," he told me, "a lot of other choices were made for me."

Now he doesn't get to choose whether he'll travel the world; he only travels the halls of the penitentiary. He doesn't have to choose what he'll eat, what he'll wear, where he'll sleep, how he'll spend his evenings, or whether or not he'll catch his son's afternoon soccer game. The Oregon State Corrections Department makes all those decisions for him.

All the decisions we make have consequences, making every decision critical. But the most prevalent problem in moral decision-making isn't knowing what is right to do, but choosing to do what we already know is right.

The apostle James said as much in his letter: "Don't, I beg you, only hear the message, but put it into practice; otherwise you are merely deluding yourselves" (James 1:22, Phillips).

It isn't knowing what to do. It's doing what we know.

Scripture says the Lord Jesus was tested in all things as we are. Does He, then, understand and empathize with this matter of hard choices? If you doubt it, come take a walk with me in a garden. You'll never doubt it again.

In the Garden of Gethsemane, the Galilean Carpenter was faced with the most dreadful choice a man has ever had to make.

Would He, in the prime of manhood, lay down His life that very day?

Would He, the One who had never sinned, wrap Himself with the putrid garments of damnation, absorbing into His body the sins of all humanity for all time?

Would He, who had known an eternity of cloudless, face-to-face intimacy within the Godhead, behold His Father's back for the first time?

Yes, He *knew* God's will. And yes, He was the Son of God. But we dare not imagine that doing the right thing in that instance was an easy decision for Jesus. The prospect before Him was so torturous and shot-through with anguish that drops of blood seeped through His skin and fell to the dusty soil as He prayed.

Hard? Yes, *cruelly* hard. His human nature and human body and human desires shrank away from the thought and screamed in His ears. But it all boiled down to this: Was He going to do His Father's will—*no matter what*—or wasn't He?

It's the same for you and me: Are we going to follow Him as Lord, or aren't we? Are we going to trust Him, or aren't we?

When I ponder this matter of following and trusting, I'm reminded of a memorable experience a few years back.

Cypress Point Golf Course in Pebble Beach, California, is one of the most scenic and beautifully-groomed courses on the planet. Stunning seascapes loom at every turn. Deer run wild. Seals play along the beach. Dolphins and whales spout and frolic just offshore. When I was presented with the opportunity to play golf at the revered course, I jumped at it.

One of the club rules at Cypress is that everyone, young or old, must play with a caddie. Even though I'd golfed for years, I'd never used one before. Truthfully, I felt kind of funny about it.

To begin with, I just play for fun, while these caddies had trailed some of the greatest legends in pro golfing. It made me feel self-conscious to have someone like that looking over my shoulder. Second, the caddie assigned to me was elderly enough to be my grandfather. With the way I hit the ball, I knew the old gentleman would be in for a lot of walking.

As we teed off on the first hole, I was so nervous that my drive went absolutely nowhere. The venerable caddie smiled.

"Don't feel too bad, son," he said. "I've seen worse shots on this hole."

That first shot was so poor that I hit a mulligan (a golfer's term for "legal cheating"). As we walked to the second shot, we spent a little time learning about each other. I discovered my caddie's name was Ed and that he was sixty-eight years old.

When we arrived at the ball I asked Ed how far he thought I was from the hole. He replied that it looked like about 163 yards to him.

"Uhh, 163 yards?"

"Yes, 163 yards."

As I mentioned, I'd had some experience playing golf, and I knew it wasn't a foot less than 185 yards. I entertained the idea that Ed had walked the course one time too many.

Ed, however, wasn't about to budge. Nor was I. I took out my 5 iron and proceeded to hit it nearly 185 yards...over the green and into a patch of rocks near the beach.

I was dumbfounded. Ed amused himself by replacing my divot.

The next hole didn't turn out much better for me. It was a long hole, and on my final shot to the green I again asked my cohort how far he thought it was.

"It's 189 yards," he replied, barely looking up from the club he was cleaning.

That did it. When he said 189 yards I knew his eyesight was faltering. There was nothing wrong with my depth perception, and it didn't look an inch over 170 to me. I hit the ball very close to 170 yards...and watched it land at least 15 yards short. Ed busied himself with polishing my putter.

My final humiliation came at the green. As we walked up to my ball, I noticed that my friends' caddies were helping them read their putts. Not wanting to seem bitter, I asked Ed which way he thought the ball would roll: to the right or to the left of the cup? Ed replied immediately that the ball would roll to the left, toward the ocean.

"They always break toward the ocean," he assured me.

Now he was mocking me. He had to be. The ball

clearly had to break to the right, because *that was the way the ground slanted.* Did the ocean have some sort of miraculous gravitational pull on my Number Three Titlest? I thought not.

I thought wrong. I missed the putt. Ed, apparently having run short of things to do to amuse himself, looked me straight in the eye.

"Son," he said, "I think you need to make a decision here, and soon. Because if you don't, it's going to be a long day for both of us. See, I have one job. Every day, I walk this course and tell people how far they have to hit the ball. That's it. That's all I do. I don't have to mow, I don't have to fertilize, and I don't have to make sandwiches at the clubhouse. I leave those things to the people who know how to do them, and they leave the guessing of yardage to me.

"I've walked this course for over fifty years and I know every tree and every blade of grass. And when I say 167 yards, I don't mean 169. What you have to do is decide if you are going to trust me or not."

With that, Ed replaced my putter in the bag and walked on to the next tee.

From that moment on, I made up my mind to trust Ed. How could I go wrong? He knew more about Cypress Point than I could learn in half a century. It makes me embarrassed to think I would second-guess that grand old caddie.

I have the same response when I think how I've tried to outguess the Lord over the years. How prideful to think I might know more about what's "best" for me at any given moment than He does. He has walked the course of this life and knows it well. *He designed it.*

Nothing we face is a surprise to Him. He's seen it all.

During the round at Cypress Point, Ed didn't offer to play the game for me, nor did he insist I do what he said. He was just offering his advice; I could choose to do what I wished. Frankly, I should never have resisted the wisdom of that seasoned professional. I didn't realize he was so experienced; I didn't realize he had caddied for Tom Watson. I guess I knew in my heart, from the beginning, he was right but, like the old song says, "I did it *my* way."

If God were our caddie, He probably wouldn't say, "Let Me hit the ball," but, "Let Me show you how." He doesn't force us to walk a certain way, but He does offer to go with us to lead us, to guide us, and help us.

As David wrote:

I will bless the LORD who has given me counsel;
My heart also instructs me in the night seasons
(Psalm 16:7).

As the Lord whispers to us:

I will instruct you and teach you
in the way you should go;
I will guide you with My eye...

Whether you turn to the right or to the left,
your ears will hear a voice behind you, saying,
"This is the way; walk in it" (Psalm 32:8; Isaiah
30:21, NIV).

The Lord doesn't demand we do what He says. He generally offers us more *wisdom* than *answers*. The Scripture doesn't say, "If you lack answers, ask." No...it says, "If you lack wisdom, ask and He'll give it." And the Lord doesn't say, "This is the answer," treating us like religious robots who don't have to think, reason, or choose for ourselves. Rather, He tends to say, "There are two roads to take, two masters to follow, two destinies to pursue. Now you choose."

When it comes to decisions, the Lord presents us with the options and then clearly lays out the consequences for each. He says, "Trust in the LORD with all your heart, and lean not on your own understanding; in all your ways acknowledge Him, and He shall direct your paths" (Proverbs 3:5,6). It's a conditional promise. If you'll trust in the Lord with "all" your heart and not lean on your own wisdom or skills, always (not sometimes) inviting Him into the process of your decision-making, then He will direct your path and show you the way. On the other hand, if you choose to willfully disobey God's Word, the results are painful and hard.

I wasn't used to trusting a caddie, so I felt I had to rely on myself. I had no idea he knew more about golf than I. Consequently, I opted to override his wisdom and do it myself. But he did know more about golf than I. All the time I was learning the pain and humiliation of disregarding his counsel.

Our daily decisions—small though they may seem to us at the time—have far-reaching impact. The enemy whispers, "What? This small compromise? It's so trivial! You can make amends later, if you need to. Go ahead and entertain that little thought. Go ahead and read that magazine. Go ahead and cut that corner. Go ahead and flirt a little. Go ahead and break that promise to your kids. You can make it up. It's not a big thing."

Yet it is. For life is made up of little turnings, little decisions. It is folly to think we can continually turn one way in all our small decisions and then tell ourselves we'll do differently when the big matters come along.

Let me give you a snapshot of a small decision. When my boys were little—probably ages six and ten—they were smitten by the fish bug. They desperately wanted to purchase and populate an aquarium. Being a pastor of a growing church, however, doesn't leave much time for fishing expeditions. But it meant so much to my little guys, that I set aside time for a family outing one Saturday morning.

Finally the big day came, and it truly was a big day. We were on the way to Fish City to look at filters, rocks, fake foliage, and fish. As I learned on the way, the boys had done their homework. They told me about freshwater fish, salt-water fish, fighting fish, puffer fish, spitting fish, and fish that make a living sucking slime off the sides of the tank. (And I thought pastoring was tough.) They wondered aloud if the store would have any Brazilian Fighting Guppies or Silver-tipped Flying Angels.

We got out of the car at Fish City and Joyce and the boys made an excited beeline for the door. I was going that way, too, but got headed off at the pass by a man from our congregation who spotted me in the parking lot. I waved my family on. This would only take a minute. But out of the corner of my eye I saw little Ron pause at the door. The expression on his face said, *Dad, you are coming in, aren't you? We are going to do this together, aren't we?* I smiled and nodded and he went on in.

Somehow, though I knew better, I allowed this man to draw me into a discussion on the fine points of a peripheral church issue. I could have excused myself. I ought to have excused myself. But I didn't.

When I finally broke away I went on into the store in time to meet my family coming out. Joyce was holding the little aquarium and the boys were clutching little water-filled bags of brightly colored fish.

Mark looked up at me. "Dad, where *were* you? We waited for you as long as we could. We wanted you to help us decide."

I'd missed that opportunity to be with them. Never again would they select fish for the first time, and there was no way to go back and do it again.

On the way home they were quiet. On the way home I grieved.

How trivial, you might say. Yet what is parenting but a hundred million small choices? And each choice affects the next. This was the first time they bought tropical fish. But how about their first Little League game? How about their first parent-teacher night? How about getting home from their first dates? How about the first time they would be rejected by a girl or challenged by a bully or tested in their faith by a cynical teacher? Would I be there for them then? Or would my choices subtly, oh-so-gradually lead me right out of their confidences, right out of their hearts, right out of their lives?

We so easily forsake responsibilities: It's easier to walk out and not look back instead of caring for a wife and children. It's easier to divorce than to trust God and make it work. It's easier to run than to stay and endure. It's easier to say yes to the social pressure of the moment than keep a promise to your kids. It's easier to abandon, to neglect, to short-cut, to quit.

Why is that? Why does "right" always seem so hard and "wrong" so easy?

To answer that question, maybe we need to go back to another garden, the Garden of Eden. That was the place where sin seemed so small and innocent in its birth. In that paradise, the tempter was in disguise—an ordinary beast of the field. The temptation was in disguise—dressed as a beautiful tree bearing luscious fruit. What could be the harm? So the tempted said, *"Not Thy will but mine be done."*

That one decision turned life into death, pleasure into pain, abundance into toil, fellowship into conflict. Critical choices are often made privately and alone, but their consequences echo down through the ages. Adam and Eve took the path of comfort, and their utopia was turned into a torment.

How, then, do we make "right" decisions?

The answer is rooted in the Garden of Gethsemane. The Second Adam was God who came to be man. In this garden, He chose the path of suffering instead of the path of comfort. On His shoulders, He bore the harvest of sin that had grown from that earlier garden. In this garden, His torment made possible our Paradise. In this garden, He made a decision and then He acted on it: *"Not My will but Thine be done."*

What He did in that garden will echo through all eternity.

The Lord always dealt with stressful situations in the same way, whether it was temptation in the wilderness or the hour of decision at Gethsemane. He made the right choices and obeyed. Why and how?

He held to His objectives. It is impossible to make difficult decisions without a sense of personal destiny. Jesus knew His divinely-appointed assignment and would not be side-tracked or seduced. His heart was fixed on the cross. Every decision He made was tested against His calling.

In order to hold to my God-given objectives, I must wear blinders, like a racehorse, that remove potential distractions from my life, for "my heart is fixed."

He heeded God's Word. Jesus didn't make decisions based on human reason, but stood firmly on the sure Word of God saying "It is written." God's Word answers questions and clears away the fog of confusion that comes from listening to too many voices.

Life can be simpler when we live in accordance with His Word. Most of the struggles in our lives are the result of not doing what we know is right. My mom's spankings certainly taught me that. If we heed God's Word, He'll fight for us, not against us.

He helped others before Himself. Many people feel used at times, but being used is different than *letting* yourself be used. Serving means unselfishly choosing to put others first without harboring bitterness, anger, or resentment. Jesus said, "No one takes My life; I give it." When you truly live for others, decisions are much easier to make. You've already decided to put others first. J. H. Jowett said, "Ministry that costs nothing accomplishes nothing."

He honored God's will. Jesus said, "I only say what I hear my Father say, and I only do what I see Him do." He restricted His decisions to the will of God. When He spoke to people, He was only saying to them what God the Father had already been saying to them.

Life can be simple, but that doesn't mean it's easy. If I resist His will, my destiny rests solely in my hands, but if I am obedient to His will, my future rests with Him.

He humbly prayed. Jesus prayed all the time. That was His custom. His faithful example is a constant reminder that the weapons of warfare at our disposal are heavenly, not worldly.

On the night before He named His twelve disciples, He climbed up onto a mountainside and talked to His Father through the night.

In Gethsemane, the night before He went to the cross, He wrestled in prayer through the long dark hours while His disciples slept.

Scripture says, "Do not be unwise, but understand what the will of the Lord is" (Ephesians 5:17). We understand it by coming before Him and saying, "Well, Father, I want Your will in this situation, but it's not clear to me what it is You want me to do." Or, "Father, I think I do understand from Your Word what Your will is, but I don't seem to have the strength or will or desire to get it done."

If we want to follow Him, we must simply spend time talking to Him and listening to Him. Our victories can be no greater than the foundation we lay in prayer. We can't afford to handicap ourselves with impotent tools. Humble prayer isn't a nicety, it's a necessity, especially when we're faced with decisions that have eternal consequences.

An old sea captain named Eleazar Hall lived in Bedford, Massachusetts, during the time of the great sailing ships. He was renowned, legendary, and revered as the most successful of all captains of the day. He worked harder, stayed out longer, and lost fewer men while catching more fish than anyone else.

Captain Hall was often asked about his uncanny ability to stay out so long without navigational equipment. He'd once been gone for two years without coming home for a point of reference.

Eleazar simply replied, "Oh, I just go up on the deck and listen to the wind and rigging. I get the drift of the sea, look up at the stars, and then set my course."

Well, times changed in Bedford. The big insurance companies moved in and said they could no longer insure the ships if the captains didn't have a certified and properly trained navigator on board. They were terrified to tell Eleazar. But to their amazement he said, "If I must, I will go and take the navigational courses."

Eleazar graduated high in his class and, having greatly missed the sea, he immediately took off for a long voyage. On the day of his return, the whole town turned out to ask him the question:

"Eleazar, how was it having to navigate with all those charts and equations?"

Eleazar sat back and let out a long, slow whistle. "Oh," he replied, "it was simply wonderful. Whenever I wanted to know my location, I'd go to my cabin, get out my charts and tables, work the equations and set my course with scientific precision. Then I'd go up on the deck and listen to the wind and rigging, get the drift of the sea, look at the stars, and go back and correct the errors that I had made in computation."

When I heard that, I prayed, *Lord, I want to know You that way. I want to go up on deck, hear Your quiet voice in my heart, consider Your eternal Word, and then go back down below and make adjustments to all those fine, logical, scientific plans I've drawn up in my head.*

It's a long way across the ocean. The way can be dark or stormy or heavy with fog and mist.

But we won't get off course or lose our bearings if we stand on deck every night with our Navigator.

126

CHAPTER NINE

Delays

Now a certain man was sick, Lazarus of Bethany, the town of Mary and her sister Martha....

Therefore the sisters sent to Him, saying, "Lord, behold, he whom You love is sick." When Jesus heard that, He said, "This sickness is not unto death, but for the glory of God, that the Son of God may be glorified through it." Now Jesus loved Martha and her sister and Lazarus. So, when He heard that he was sick, He stayed two more days in the place where He was....

After that He said to them, "Our friend Lazarus sleeps, but I go that I may wake him up." Then His disciples said, "Lord, if he sleeps he will get well.... Then Jesus said to them plainly,

"Lazarus is dead. And I am glad for your sakes that I was not there, that you may believe. Nevertheless let us go to him"

So when Jesus came, He found that he had already been in the tomb four days.... Then Martha, as soon as she heard that Jesus was coming, went and met Him, but Mary was sitting in the house. Now Martha said to Jesus, "Lord, if You had been here, my brother would not have died" (John 11:1,3-7,11-12, 14-15,17,20-21).

I've *always* had trouble waiting for Christmas.

I get so excited thinking about December 25th that visions of sugar plums begin to dance in my head before Labor Day. Some folks get upset because the stores start pushing lights and tinsel before Halloween. Not me; I'm ready by the Fourth of July.

I know one boy (who will remain unnamed) who couldn't stand the delay any more. He was so anxious to explore the mysteries under the tree that he sneaked in one night and opened every gift he had. Then, after surveying his treasures, he rewrapped them all and put them back under the tree. That little guy had a terrible Christmas. There was no anticipation. No surprises. He couldn't fake it and everything was ruined.

One little family in Bethany a couple thousand years ago endured a fever of anticipation. Only they weren't waiting for Christmas, they were waiting for Christ. They weren't waiting for gifts, they were waiting for the Gift-Giver. And when He didn't come, when He didn't seem to care, it broke their hearts.

Most delays are simply a matter of inconvenience... waiting through a traffic jam...waiting for a check in the mail...waiting for a tardy paperboy...waiting for your car at the shop. For Mary, Martha, and Lazarus, however, it was an issue of life and death.

Beyond that, it was an issue of love.

What could Jesus have been *doing* that was more important than helping His dear friends in their hour of deepest anguish? They had thought one simple little note—*"Lord, behold, he whom You love is sick"*—would have brought Him running.

It hadn't.

Inevitably, they were left with their questions. Why would He make them wait when He knew how hard it would be on them? He knew they would be hurting, so why linger? He had the power to act, so why didn't He?

For that household in Bethany, life came to a standstill. Everything froze. Martha, always so concerned about the details of running an efficient domestic operation, probably let everything go. Dishes stacked up in the sink. Dust bunnies piled up in the corners. Clothes heaped up in the hamper. Mary, who loved to sit at the Lord's feet, sat alone in her sorrow. A thousand times a day, she glanced down the road in front of their house. No road ever looked so empty.

That's a kind of waiting that goes deeper than inconvenience and surface impatience. It's a profound kind of waiting that pulls at the heart like a fish hook embedded in flesh. Like waiting to see if you're among those who will get a pink slip on the following Friday...or waiting for the results of a critical lab test...or waiting for a wandering spouse to come home...or

waiting by the bedside of a little one with a high fever...
or waiting for word about a teenager who failed to return
from a hunting trip.

If you've ever done *that* kind of waiting, you'll
never worry as much about the trivial stuff again. If
you've ever done that kind of waiting, you know what it
means to wonder with Mary, *Where is the Lord? Why
doesn't He come? Why, oh, why does He delay?*

Imagine yourself desperate to get to an appointment
across town. And you find yourself waiting at a stoplight
that never, never changes. The light burns red like an
unblinking eye and traffic goes by and you never move.

Imagine your child being struck by a car out in front
of your house. You carry that precious bundle into the
living room, dial 9-1-1, and the phone just rings and rings
and rings. No one ever answers.

It must have been like that for the two sisters in
Bethany. They dialed 9-1-1 and the Lord didn't pick up
the phone. In the throes of their frustration and grief,
they were about to learn a crucial password to life in
Christ. It's *patience.*

When I'm impatient, it's usually because I'm not getting my way. If my schedule isn't adopted or my plans
aren't accepted, I get uneasy. Maybe a little testy. Some
people give Tylenol more time to work than the Lord. Some
people are born with red hair, some with black hair, some
with brown eyes, some with green eyes, but none of us are
born with patience and *none* of us are fond of delays.

The only exception I can think of to this aspect of
the human condition would be during courtship...when
something strange happens to the space/time continuum.

When I was dating Joyce, I wore a beat up, weary-faced Timex with a phony alligator band. It had taken a lot of lickin's, and wasn't always tickin'. But none of that mattered. When I was with Joyce, it didn't need to keep good time. It didn't need to be reliable. It didn't matter if it stopped altogether. In that girl's company, I *wanted* time to stop. It didn't even trouble me if she was a little late getting ready for our date. Waiting was no problem. It simply meant she wasn't quite done making herself even more beautiful...just for me.

When you get married, something seems to happen to that insulating layer of patience and grace. What was once an awed sense of wonder and anticipation over what she might be putting on or how she might be fixing her hair turns into a honk of the car horn and a what-took-you-so-long-glance when she "finally" comes through the front door.

"Long-suffering" may be a fruit of the Holy Spirit in our lives, but any apple farmer or lemon rancher or vineyard keeper will tell you the same thing: fruit takes time; fruit takes cultivation; fruit takes careful nurturing to come to maturity; fruit has to be *grown*. There may be instant apple sauce and instant lemon pudding, but there are no such things as instant apples or lemons. Fruit needs rain and sunlight and fertilizer and bug protection and pruning and tender loving care.

So does the fruit of patience. It can't be whipped up like instant pudding. It is something God *grows* in you as you walk with Him through sunlight and storm and respond to those things He brings into your life. Paul said to the Philippians, "I have learned in whatever state I am, to be content." The key words in that statement are *I have learned.*

The curriculum God uses to impart this crucial aspect of learning is trials:

> My brethren, count it all joy when you fall into various trials, knowing that the testing of your faith produces patience. But let patience have its perfect work, that you may be perfect and complete, lacking nothing (James 1:2-4).

The emphasis here isn't so much on the trial or the test, but on whether we will *allow* the season of testing. James says, "Let patience have its perfect work." In other words, *don't try to shortcut the growing season.* From Noah waiting for a cloud, to Hannah waiting for a child, to Habakkuk waiting for justice, to the disciples waiting for the Spirit at Pentecost, men and women who experienced God's power and provision had to exercise patience.

God's plan for possessing patience is time, as He weaves us through a series of events to strip us of the belief that our needs and desires must be met on our own timetable.

I have wept with people who love the Lord with all their heart. They're faithful servants and stewards, but are facing financial pressure, the loss of their home and things they hold dear. "Why?" they ask me. "Where is this God who says He loves His children, who says He'll bless His people and that He'll never leave them and never forsake them? Why hasn't He come? Where is He? What is He doing?"

He's in the same place, doing the same thing today He was doing when Mary and Martha needed Him. He's being God. And one of the jobs of God is to perfect His people. That is an immeasurably Good Thing. But it takes time. And it requires endurance.

If you've had children, you've probably been through the routine of "growth marks" on the child's bedroom closet wall. Remember those? Our son used his closet for basically two reasons: one, it was his own personal, private museum and art gallery. He liked to draw his own renditions of twenty-first century war games. He also used his closet to monitor his growth. At one point, he insisted we measure him *every night* to see how much he had grown each day. He had a hard time realizing that growth takes time. Patience wasn't a lesson he had yet learned.

Most valuable things take time. Healthy marriages take time. Developing a successful business takes time. Maturing in Christ takes time. Raising children fit to turn loose on society certainly takes time!

Our two young sons used to pack up each summer to spend some time with their grandma and grandpa in Louisiana. My wife and I always panicked just before those vacations. We were so anxious that the boys be joys and not burdens. After all, the South requires "yes, Ma'ams" and "no, Ma'ams" and all the little refinements that Northern children (even well-mannered ones) don't have occasion to learn—unless their parents grew up below the Mason-Dixon line.

A day or so before they'd leave, we'd say, "Now guys, when Grandma says, 'Would you like to eat?' then what do you say?"

They would usually say what comes naturally to young boys, and it was not, "Yes Ma'am." A crash course in Southern etiquette didn't work, because then it was only in their heads, not their hearts. I knew when Grandma said, "Honey, would you like some peas?" they'd point to the corner of the plate and say, "Yeah, just dump a load here."

Those gracious, considerate, gentlemanly traits are learned by patient, faithful care. For parents, it means paying the price to make the time and do the work necessary to teach them.

If we learn patience by living, then what things in life are we being taught? God's timetable for us is always backed up by divine design. When God waits, delays, or lingers, He has a plan, and the plan is to teach us something about Himself, His heart, or ourselves.

Mary and Martha *thought* they knew the Lord, but this episode would teach them volumes more about their divine Friend.

1. The Lord taught them about His love.

It's much easier to be patient when we actually believe the person we're waiting on really loves us. Believing God always has our best interest at heart eases our apprehension and fear. Jesus loved Mary, Martha, and Lazarus. There was no question in the Lord's mind about that.

"Lord, behold, he whom You love is sick...."

"Now Jesus loved Martha and her sister and Lazarus...."

But if He loved them, why make them wait?

The real test of your love for the Lord is endurance and trust, believing even when circumstances scream out that God has forsaken you.

I am deeply moved by the patience and persevering faith of a woman I know who has been so kind, forgiving, and strong, while watching her husband struggle. Most people I know would have thrown up their hands and run long ago. But not this woman. She seems capable of carrying more and persevering longer than anyone I've ever seen.

But the proverbial "last straw" came just a few weeks ago. In *anybody's* book this would have been the thing that finally slammed, padlocked, and boarded over the door. But just when she knew she couldn't go on any further, the Lord spoke to her.

Let us go a little longer, He said.

Because He said "us," she drew fresh strength. It would be the Lord and her.

Guess what occupies the heart of God. Guess what dominates His day. Guess what fills the "To Do" column of His celestial Daytimer.

You.

When someone loves you, they live for you, and they think about you all the time. Never doubt that it was love that stayed the feet of the Lord Jesus. The delay in going to Bethany was set in a context of love. And so are the delays in your life.

2. He taught them about His timing.

Martha said to the Lord in John 11:21, "Lord, if You had been here, my brother would not have died." Though God is above time and unbound by time, He still keeps a heavenly timetable. The Scripture uses expressions such as, "in due time," "in the fullness of time," and "at the accepted time." It means not a moment before or after the time God intends.

One commentator highlights an ancient Jewish belief about death: Jews, he maintained, believed that for three days the soul hovered about the sepulcher, anxious to reenter the body. By waiting, Jesus taught them that the

Father has the power to bestow eternal life. Had He come earlier, it could have been argued that He performed no miracle, and did nothing at all. I agree with the old adage that God may seem slow, but He's never late.

The Lord has an amazing "deferred benefit" plan. Simeon waited three-quarters of a century for the coming of the infant Christ. Abraham waited twenty-five years for the birth of Isaac, and Joseph waited thirteen years for deliverance from slavery and prison. The benefits of trusting the Lord may be deferred, but they're always worth the wait.

3. He taught them about His purpose.

The sisters in Bethany said, "Lord, if You had come when we called, Lazarus would be alive and everything would be fine." Some people believe that silence and indifference are synonyms. They're not. Just because the Lord doesn't seem to be saying anything doesn't mean He isn't saying something. Claude Updike, a saintly missionary now home with the Lord, used to say, "When you walk as an obedient, faithful soldier of the cross and you lose something or something is taken away, never worry. God always has something better to give you or to teach you."

The purpose of the Lord here was to show Mary, Martha, Lazarus—and eventually you and me—that He was the Resurrection and the Life. Yes, He could have healed Lazarus and they would have been thrilled. Yes, He could have come earlier and saved them the pain and misery of death and they would have been grateful. But if Jesus Christ had not honored His Father's timetable, they would never have learned He could raise people from the dead.

They would not have realized He is the Lord of Life.

There's a vast difference between God's purpose

and our purpose. God's delays reveal His plan. Had Jesus raised Lazarus earlier, an earthly purpose would have been achieved, but not God's purpose.

4. He taught them something about themselves.

Impatience is always self-centered. Always in a hurry. Always agitated. Always doubting and second-guessing. Patience shouldn't be characterized by inactivity, resignation, or defeat, but a positive, persevering faith that remains active when what you're waiting for has yet to come to pass.

God uses delays to force our failures, weaknesses, and lack of faith into the open. We want everything to look good. God desires a deeper work in us, dealing with the dead things that need the touch of His resurrection power. Some people contend for restoration when what they should be asking for is resurrection. There's a difference. Restoration can make a bad thing better, but it can't bring a dead thing back to life.

A pastor friend of mine told me about a couple in his congregation who were having marital problems. They weren't doing very well; in fact, things were getting worse. Neither one was honest or humble enough to take the first step toward reconciling.

Then they had a vision. I know...speaking of dreams and visions stretches some people, but that's what happened, and it went like this: They were gardeners who went out to check on their garden. Nothing was growing. They looked down and saw a very small hole in the ground. They went over, got down on their knees and peeked through the small hole. They were shocked at what they saw. Underneath the garden, it was filled with deadly and horrible-looking creatures.

They said, "Lord, what's that?"

"It's your marriage," He told them. "On top and on the outside, everything looks good. But deep down, underneath, there's something horribly wrong. There's no fragrance, no fruitfulness, no blessing."

Let the Lord lead you through circumstances that will reveal the areas in your life that need work. If there's something you need to learn, let Him teach you.

God's primary work in our lives is to develop faith in us, increasing our faith so that we can do a greater work. If you want to evaluate a man or woman's virtues, don't scrutinize his or her life on a good day. Wait until the pressure's on. Wait until weariness sets in. Wait until difficulties mount. Adversity reveals the true nature of a person's walk. It's in the heat of the battle that we discover who the warriors are.

Luis Palau tells of a missionary mother with a precious, mentally-handicapped child. When this cheerful little lad ate, it was standard procedure for him to spill his milk and generally make a mess.

On one occasion, he spilled *a lot* of food, and it went *everywhere.* The boy's mother was an extraordinarily kind, patient, and loving woman. She cleaned up after these food fiascoes again and again with grace and patience. But on this day, it was more than even she could handle. One lonely flying banana touched off an explosion.

After she blew up, the little boy looked up into her face, smiled broadly, and began to sing out loud a song he'd heard on the radio: "I beg your pardon, I never promised you a rose garden." Her anger and impatience vanished just that fast, and the two of them enjoyed a good long laugh together.

Life isn't a rose garden, and none of us have been promised that. Some say that spiritual depth comes from God's Word, while others say a well-rounded Christian is shaped by worship, fellowship, and stewardship. James says maturity and spiritual growth come from letting patience have her perfect work, testing every virtue and challenging every weakness. Patience makes a trip around our life and looks for any weaknesses and any flaws. No mature saint can say that his stature in Christ has come without tribulations and trials and agony over delays and prayers that seem to go unanswered.

Roger Simms had just left the military and was anxious to take his uniform off once and for all. He was hitchhiking home, and his heavy duffel bag made the trip even more arduous than hitchhiking normally is. Flashing his thumb to an oncoming car, he lost hope when he saw that it was a shiny, black, expensive car, so new that it had a temporary license in the back window...hardly the type of car that would stop for a hitchhiker.

But to his amazement, the car stopped and the passenger door opened. He ran toward the car, placed his duffel carefully in the back, and slid into the leather-covered front seat. He was greeted by the friendly smile of a handsome older gentleman with distinguished gray hair and a deep tan.

"Hello, son. Are you on leave or are you going home for good?"

"I just got out of the army, and I'm going home for the first time in several years," answered Roger.

"Well, you're in luck if you're going to Chicago," smiled the man.

"Not quite that far," said Roger, "but my home is on

the way. Do you live there, Mister?"

"Hanover. Yes, I have a business there." And with that, they were on their way.

After giving each other brief life histories, and talking about everything under the sun, Roger (who was a Christian) felt a strong compulsion to witness to Mr. Hanover about Christ. But witnessing to an elder, wealthy businessman who obviously had everything he could ever want was a scary prospect indeed. Roger kept putting it off, but as he neared his destination, he realized it was now or never.

"Mr. Hanover," began Roger, "I would like to talk to you about something very important." He then proceeded to explain the way of salvation, ultimately asking Mr. Hanover if he would like to receive Christ as his Savior. To Roger's astonishment, the big car pulled over to the side of the road; Roger thought for a moment that Mr. Hanover was about to throw him out. Then a strange and wonderful thing happened: the businessman bowed his head to the steering wheel and began to cry, affirming that he did in fact want to accept Christ into his heart. He thanked Roger for talking to him, saying that, "This is the greatest thing that has ever happened to me." He then dropped Roger at his house and traveled on toward Chicago.

Five years went by, and Roger Simms married, had a child, and started a business of his own. One day, while packing for a business trip to Chicago, he came across a small, gold-embossed business card which Mr. Hanover had given him years earlier.

When Roger arrived in Chicago, he looked up Hanover Enterprises, and found it to be located downtown in a very tall and important-looking building. The receptionist told him that it would be impossible to see

Mr. Hanover, but that if he was an old friend he would be able to see Mrs. Hanover. A little disappointed, he was led into a poshly-decorated office where a woman in her fifties was sitting at a huge oak desk.

She extended her hand. "You knew my husband?"

Roger explained how Mr. Hanover had been kind enough to give him a ride back home.

A look of interest passed across her face. "Can you tell me what date that was?"

"Sure," said Roger. "It was May 7th, five years ago, the day I was discharged from the army."

"And did anything special happen on your ride...anything unusual?"

Roger hesitated. Should he mention giving his witness? Had it been some source of contention between the two, which resulted in a marital breakup or separation? But once again, he felt the prompting of the Lord to be truthful. "Mrs. Hanover, your husband accepted the Lord into his heart that day. I explained the gospel message to him, and he pulled to the side of the road and wept, and then chose to pray a prayer of salvation."

Suddenly, she began to sob uncontrollably. After several minutes she regained enough control to explain what had happened: "I grew up in a Christian home, but my husband did not. I had prayed for my husband's salvation for many years, and I believed God would save him. But just after he let you out of his car, on May 7th, he passed away in a horrible head-on collision. He never arrived home. I thought God had not kept His promise, and I stopped living for the Lord five years ago because I blamed Him for not keeping His word."

I can identify with Mrs. Hanover. Perhaps you can, too. There are long, lonely stretches in life when it seems as if God has simply become indifferent toward our plight and bored or apathetic about our fervent prayers.

It's like staring at tightly-wrapped, mysterious, and unavailable presents under a tree. As time goes on and hope stretches thin, we begin to wonder if God really *has* any gifts for us.

Maybe you've been waiting a long time for situations to change in your life. You've been waiting for a change in your health, in your relationships, in your spouse, in your children, in your job, in your finances, in your spiritual life. And it seems the delay goes on forever. It seems Christmas will never come. It seems the light will never change. It seems you've dialed the Lord's 9-1-1 line a thousand times and He's never answered.

Mary and Martha know all about that. They watched their brother weaken and fail. His life slipped through their fingers like sand and they couldn't stop it and the Lord didn't come.

But then He did come. And it was too late. But it wasn't too late. Because what He had in mind was something so far beyond their thoughts and experience and hopes and dreams that they didn't even think to ask for it.

It was a Very Good Thing wrapped in a Very Bad Thing.

And He delivered it Himself...right on time.

He always does.

CHAPTER TEN

Burdens

Now from the sixth hour until the ninth hour there was darkness over all the land. And about the ninth hour Jesus cried out with a loud voice, saying, "Eli, Eli, lama sabachthani?" that is, "My God, My God, why have You forsaken Me?" Some of those who stood there, when they heard that, said, "This Man is calling for Elijah!" Immediately one of them ran and took a sponge, filled it with sour wine and put it on a reed, and gave it to Him to drink. The rest said, "Leave Him alone; let us see if Elijah will come to save Him." And Jesus cried out again with a loud voice, and yielded up His spirit (Matthew 27:45-50).

As they were growing up, our sons used to spend their summers with Grandma and Grandpa down in Louisiana bayou country. We're talking fried okra, purple hull peas, and Blackened Cajun Everything.

Nestled at a juncture of three lakes, Grandma and Grandpa's house was a perfect setting for two little guys starved for adventure. Disney World had nothing on this place. There were motorcycles, horses, birds, bugs, tree forts, snakes, and opossums. It even had Hey-Boy, a sure-enough alligator who stuck a bumpy snout out of the swamp when called and willingly feasted on Oscar Mayer wieners. In Shreveport there were more things for two boys to do before seven in the morning than in most other places all day.

I can remember looking out the big front window one misty bayou morning and what I saw became one of those permanent snapshots glued in the mind's photo album. I can see it at this moment, many miles and years distant, in vivid Kodacolor detail.

Dressed in T-shirts and jeans, the boys were making their way down to "The Barge," their affectionate name for a square, ungainly, twelve-foot fishing boat. They were manfully trying to haul their share of the gear for a fishing expedition with Grandpa.

Lurching across the yard, over the gravel driveway, and through the grass, the boys staggered under a load of bamboo poles, bait buckets, tackle boxes, nets, gas cans for the old Evinrude, and Grandma's ample lunch basket. They were weighed down with so much paraphernalia you could hardly see them. They looked like two moving piles. Every few feet one of them had to circle back for something dropped before floundering on again after the other one—which made for a curious, circular pattern all the way down to the black water.

As I stood at that window watching my sons, I found myself thinking, *Wouldn't it be great if fishing gear was the only burden those little guys would have to worry about as they were growing up?* Even as I watched them putt-putt away from shore into the hazy summer morning, I knew it wouldn't—couldn't—be that way. Carrying burdens is part of the job description for living on the planet. They would have their share.

But what would they do with those burdens?

Where would they turn when the burdens came?

Would they discover the Good Thing about the Bad Thing of too-heavy loads?

From time to time we've all staggered under weights too difficult to bear. And I'm not talking about picnic baskets and bait buckets. I'm talking about heavy emotional freight that crushes the soul. At one point in his pilgrimage, David penned these words in his spiritual journal: "My guilt has overwhelmed me like a burden too heavy to bear" (Psalm 38:4, NIV).

Like David, we too may be overwhelmed by sin. Overwhelmed by guilt. Overwhelmed by grief and circumstances and worry and discouragement.

We'd like to believe we're built to carry the weight of the world on our shoulders. We tell ourselves there are few things we can't handle and few things we can't do. We cling to a stubborn streak when it comes to asking for help. It's that Rambo or Wonder Woman mentality that rises up in each of us and says: "We'll take care of it ourselves." But deep down, all of us know that trying to carry too much leads to hernias of the soul. There's a limit to what we can pack on our frail human shoulders.

I've been told that a llama will refuse to carry a pound more than it figures it should. If it thinks it ought to pack sixty-five pounds, it will not tolerate sixty-six. It just flat *won't*. Try it, and the animal will drop to its knees. Until you lift off that offending pound, kiss your packing trip good-bye.

You and I fall on our knees sometimes, too. And not always by choice. Sometimes we crumple under the crushing weight of burdens we've tried to carry but are simply too much for us.

I can still remember the day I met Alex. Her stooped shoulders, bent head, and downcast eyes told her life story without words. This young woman had been living her own personal nightmare of sin, shame, guilt, and grief. By the time I met her, she had reached her "load limit."

Alex had tried to run from the burdens of her past, but found no place of rest and no place to hide. There was no drug strong enough to eliminate the pain, and never enough alcohol to quench the dark memories. Her life reminded me of the story of B'rer Rabbit and the Tar Baby. B'rer Fox had set out to trap the wily hare, and when B'rer Rabbit tried to take matters into his own hands, the enemy's plan worked to perfection. B'rer Rabbit became stuck, and the more he struggled to get away from the black, gooey glob, the more stuck he became and the more covered he was, until he felt so heavy he could hardly move. He ended up looking like the Tar Baby himself.

That was Alex. The more she tried to shake herself free of the sticky, heavy goo of sin, the more it permeated her life. It didn't take a rocket scientist to see she had weakened to the point of going under from the weight of it.

People had been telling Alex not to worry about her plight. Counselors assured her she would feel better in time. "Time will heal everything," they said.

Really? Can time heal everything? Can time fix a burned-out light bulb? Will time repair a broken window or a flat tire? Absolutely not. Wait until you're an old man or woman and the cold air will still whistle through the broken pane. Keep riding long enough on a flat tire and it will bend the wheel. Delaying repairs won't help. Nor will time heal the sins of our past, or remove our burdens of guilt and shame. They must be dealt with.

Alex honestly tried everything. She tried to run. She tried turning to others. She did everything she knew to do.

So what can we say to someone like Alex, so overwhelmed with the burden of sin? What hope can we give? What message can we offer? What do *you* do when the burdens you face are too much to bear? What do you do when the scales of your life show you're on overload? It's human nature to run from our troubles, but can you run far enough? And if you do run, can you forget about it when you get there?

I think the psalmist said it best:

My heart is in anguish within me;
the terrors of death assail me.
Fear and trembling have beset me;
horror has overwhelmed me.
I said, "Oh, that I had the wings of a dove!
I would fly away and be at rest—
I would flee far away

and stay in the desert.   *Selah.*
I would hurry to my place of shelter,
far from the tempest and storm
(Psalm 55:4-8, NIV).

The truth is you *can* fly away. Delta Airlines can take you to one of a thousand destinations. United will vault you deep into their friendly skies in a way the psalmist would have never dreamed. But no matter. Even at 35,000 feet you won't find escape from loads you carry in your heart.

When we talk about the Bad Thing of burdens, our minds immediately shift to tangible things such as financial stress, wounded personal relationships, or maybe the pain of a wandering, rebellious child. Those are weighty enough, but there are other kinds of burdens, the kind that have eternal consequences linked to them such as sin, guilt, and hopelessness.

I'm thinking of people such as Marilyn Monroe, who said before her death, "I can't take it anymore." And what about Janis Joplin and Jimi Hendrix, the renowned rock stars? They seemed to have everything by the world's standards but, in the end, felt as if they had nothing at all. And then, of course, there's Elvis Presley who, before his death, said he'd give a million dollars for a moment's peace and rest.

Just before he shot and killed himself, Ernest Hemingway said, "There is no remedy for anything in my life. Death is a sovereign remedy for all misfortune. I live tonight in a vacuum that is as lonely as a radio when the batteries are dead and there is no current to plug into."

Burdens will drain you. Burdens will bury you. None of us is built to carry very much. Scripture says there are burdens we must carry and burdens only the Lord can carry. Knowing the difference is everything because the cares of life can crush the very life and joy out of us. When you pile on enough trouble, everyone will cave in.

For my friend, Alex, the load finally got so heavy she couldn't carry it another step. The awful weight of it finally forced her to her knees.

And somewhere, the angels cheered.

I was with Alex when she prayed, "Father, help me. I've done everything I know to do, gone everywhere I know to go, talked to everyone I know to talk to. But, Lord, if You don't change me, I'm *always* going to be this way."

It was the Bad Thing of that unbearable burden she carried that brought her to the cross, to Christ.

So what brings people to the Lord? Burdens.

What brings people to the cross? Burdens.

What brings people who wander from the Lord or scrape by in their own strength back to the Source of forgiveness and enabling and comfort and help? Burdens.

One of the most difficult times in my life was when my wife, Joyce, fell gravely ill. She'd *always* been healthy. A petite, cute little thing who never seemed to have so much as a hangnail or a headache. We noticed she'd been losing weight, but it had been very gradual. Because she's not a complainer and never talks about herself, I all but forgot about it.

One weekend our little family got away from the city to spend a couple of days at a resort near Mt. Hood. I had a fun day with the boys while Joyce relaxed and rested on the couch. I fell into an exhausted sleep that night, but woke up suddenly at 2:00 A.M. Joyce was tossing in the bed, moaning softly.

I reached over and put my hand on her. "You okay?"

"Yes," she whispered. "I'm so sorry I woke you up."

Is that ridiculous? But that's her. That's exactly what she'd say. She's hurting, but worried whether I'm going to get in my full night's rest. We prayed together, but neither of us slept much that night.

In the morning I got up, looked out the window and saw the mountain in the distance and the tree-filled hillside, and thanked the Lord for letting us have these wonderful days together as a family. When I came back into our bedroom I made some cute remark like, "When do you think you might wake up, Snow White?"

Snow White forced a smile and tried to get up. But she couldn't. She was too weak to even lift her head. She could hardly speak, and with a cold slap of alarm I realized she was struggling just to *breathe*.

I called the doctor. "Get her to the hospital immediately," he told me. "I'll meet you there."

Our young sons helped load the car, but no one said much. Then I picked her up—so light, so frail—and carefully carried her to the car. In hindsight, I now realize she couldn't have weighed over seventy-eight pounds. *How could I have been so blind?*

When we arrived at the hospital, they rushed her into intensive care. The doctor was grim.

"Pastor," he said, "I'll tell you right out. It doesn't look good."

After running a battery of tests, they determined she had diabetes. And by now there were serious complications. *Diabetes?* There was no history of diabetes in Joyce's family. The diagnosis was a total shock.

And me? I felt like Mt. Hood had just descended between my shoulder blades. Your mind races at times like that. *What would it be like without Joyce?* I couldn't imagine. Life would be black-and-white; shades of gray instead of color. Joyce is like the sunshine to our family. She's always bright and cheery, always warm, always ready for fun, and you just don't want to exist without her. We didn't even want to try.

I had carried a lot of things in my life, but nothing like this. I knew there were lots of things I could handle—and this wasn't one of them.

As they worked on Joyce, the doctor excused me. I went home to explain to our boys what had happened. We talked about everything and then prayed together. I tried to get them to sleep, but this was going to be a very long night. Lying in bed, I could hear the boys down the hall, weeping, missing their mom already.

I learned one very Good Thing on that very bad night.

Some burdens are too heavy to bear. This was way too big for me. Ridiculously large. This was a *God-sized* burden. Like a stubborn llama, I went right to my knees and didn't budge.

Lord, I remember praying, *I just want to remind You that I'm human. Just blood and flesh and bone and a little gristle. And this thing—this is too big for me. This is something I can't get my shoulders under. This is a burden too heavy for me to bear.*

The Good Thing about the Bad Thing of burdens is that when you feel the weight of them, they cause you to run to the Lord. Until you do, you'll continue to shuffle and stagger along with the weight digging into your heart. I had ample opportunity in the weeks and months of

Joyce's slow recovery to learn that lesson again and again.

The fact is, you won't come to the cross for salvation until you feel poor and worthless and unable to save yourself. You won't push off your heavy weights onto the Lord's willing shoulders until you stumble and can't get up again.

In a moment of deep distress, David wrote:

Hear my cry, O God; attend to my prayer.
From the end of the earth I will cry to You,
when my heart is overwhelmed;
lead me to the rock that is higher than I.
For You have been a shelter for me
(Psalm 61:1-3).

Until our hearts ARE overwhelmed, many of us will NOT come to the great Rock seeking shelter.

But we don't have to carry our load of sin and guilt and shame, *because Someone already did.*

The LORD has laid on Him the iniquity of us all.... He Himself bore our sins in His body on the cross, that we might die to sin and live to righteousness (Isaiah 53:6; 1 Peter 2:24, NASB).

We don't have to carry our load of care, worry, and sorrow, *because Someone already is.*

Surely He has borne our griefs and carried our sorrows... Cast your burden on the LORD, and He shall sustain you... Casting all your care upon Him, for He cares for you (Isaiah 53:4; Psalm 55:22; 1 Peter 5:7).

We don't have to stagger under the load of anxiety and fear for the future *because we rest in His very hands.*

Fear not, for I am with you;
Be not dismayed, for I am your God.
I will strengthen you,
Yes, I will help you,
I will uphold you with My righteous right hand....
[You] have been upheld by Me from birth,
[You] have been carried from the womb:
Even to your old age, I am He,
And even to gray hairs I will carry you!
I have made, and I will bear;
Even I will carry, and will deliver you
(Isaiah 41:10;46:3-4).

Burdens *belong* at Calvary. There's no sinner He can't save. There's no burden He can't carry. There's no sickness He can't heal. There's no problem He can't solve. There's no bondage He can't deliver. Some people worry about bothering God with little things—as if some things are too insignificant to trouble Him with. What a limited view of our heavenly Father! Would you, as a parent, scoff at a festering splinter in your little boy's finger? Would you turn away in disgust from your little girl suffering with a grain of sand in her eye? Remember, this is the God who has not only counted every hair on your head, He has *numbered* them. He notices when number 15,663 is out of place or lost. He takes note every time the cat next door to you catches a sparrow.

It's not a question of the size of your load, it's a question of the bent of your heart. Is He really your Lord? Is He really your Best Friend? Is He really your Rock and your Hiding Place and your Refuge? If He is, you'll bring *everything* to Him; you'll find yourself at the foot of the cross a thousand times a day.

When you think about it, it's not your load He wants

anyway. It's *you.* Just you. As close as He can bring you to His heart. As close as He can draw you into His arms. He'll carry your load, all right, because He's carrying *you.*

A missionary from Guatemala told me about driving his little truck high up in the mountains. The Indians in that area haul heavy, bulky loads on their backs when they go to market at Chi Chi Castenango. Once, while driving to the mission church, he passed an old Indian man walking along the side of the road with an impossibly heavy load of pottery on his back. He knew the man was still a long way from the market, so he stopped to offer him a ride. Though the old man had never ridden in a vehicle before, he silently climbed up into the back of the pickup with his load.

After driving several miles, the missionary looked back and saw the little man squatting in the pickup with the load still on his back.

The missionary pulled over and stepped out to talk to his passenger. "You can take the load off your back," he told him gently. "The truck will carry the load for you."

It's true. Loads down here on this old planet can get awfully heavy. Then just when the load gets heavy the pathway gets steep. Then just when the path gets steep we turn our ankle. Then just when we turn our ankle we hear the bear coming up behind us.

It's time to get into the truck, and leave the load-bearing to Him.

He'd love nothing better than your company.

CHAPTER ELEVEN

Death

There came a man named Jairus, and he was a ruler of the synagogue. And he fell down at Jesus' feet and begged Him to come to his house, for he had an only daughter about twelve years of age, and she was dying.

...Someone came from the ruler of the synagogue's house, saying to him, "Your daughter is dead. Do not trouble the Teacher." But when Jesus heard it, He answered him, saying, "Do not be afraid; only believe" (Luke 8:41-42,49-50).

"Let not your heart be troubled; you believe in God, believe also in Me. In My Father's house are many mansions; if it were not so, I would have told you. I go to prepare a place for you" (John 14:1-2).

Inasmuch then as the children have partaken of flesh and blood, He Himself likewise shared in the same, that through death He might destroy him who had the power of death, that is, the devil, and release those who through fear of death were all their lifetime subject to bondage (Hebrews 2:14-15).

I remember an episode of "Gilligan's Island" in which Gilligan, after botching yet *another* rescue attempt, decided to stage his own death to save himself further shame and embarrassment. After leaving his hat on top of a pool of quicksand, he went to live on the other side of the island, hoping he wouldn't ever have to face the other castaways again.

But curiosity got the better of him.

On the day of his "funeral," he just couldn't help himself. He crept back to watch the ceremony from the treetops, curious to learn exactly how much his friends missed him.

Perhaps we all have a secret desire, in some dark corner of our minds, to know what our funeral service would be like. How many people would come? Would police be needed to direct traffic and provide crowd control? Where would they hold the service? In a small chapel? A large sanctuary? The Astro Dome? Would there be lots of flowers? Would people be whispering bitter words among themselves, or would they stand and speak with choked voices and tear-filled eyes?

We all like to believe we'd be sorely missed, but who knows? One thing, however, is certain: All our questions about death will eventually be answered.

The words to the old hymn are still on target: *"There's no hidin' place down here."* Can we hide from disaster? Can we hide from disease? Can we hide from death?

No, none of us can. Not even the most wealthy and powerful.

Multi-billionaire Howard Hughes wanted to hide from death. Toward the end of his days, he secreted himself away in a germ-free environment, not allowing anyone to come into his presence without rubber gloves and a face mask. But Death, the intruder, came through the locked door without knocking and that was that.

No one is exempt from mortality, and not one of us can evade it. For all of us, life is as fragile as a freshly-blown bubble.

And only Gilligan gets to peek down from the treetops.

In my mind, there are several categories, or classifications of death. Gilligan knew a thing or two about dying emotionally; that's when you make a terminally stupid blunder and "embarrass yourself to death."

There is a second way in which we die; it's called dying to self. That means saying no to that part of you that wants its own way, the part that seeks glory and hungers for attention. As Paul says, it is dying daily to worldly passions, selfishness, and carnal pleasures.

Then, of course, there is physical death. It is no respecter of persons, and it takes roll every day. The book of Job calls death "the king of terrors." It's terrifying because we know so little about it. It's frightening because of the pain that surrounds it and the desolation it leaves in its wake.

Several years ago, a television newswoman named Julie Arguinzoni visited the L.A. County Morgue to tape a story on the tragic deaths due to drug abuse. The newswoman was shown into the room known as the "Refrigerator," a giant chamber used to store unidentified "John and Jane Doe" corpses until identified. What she saw there shocked and sickened her. Stacked like cord wood lay 650 unclaimed human bodies—mostly young boys and girls—picked up off the streets, in bars, or motel rooms. The bodies, she was told, were held for six months. If still unclaimed, they were cremated.

As she left the Refrigerator, Julie said later she heard a voice in her mind, like the voice of Satan.

"These," it whispered, "are my trophies!"

Death has its own agenda and timeline. It possesses both young and old, cherished and abandoned, wise and foolish, good and bad. It doesn't pick and choose. It doesn't care about age, race, gender, or political persuasion. It is not intimidated by stature, influence, or possessions. And it can strike utterly without warning.

A friend of mine told me about a woman who carried her weekly laundry into her local laundromat. Suddenly a car on the street out front veered off the road, smashed through a great pane-glass window, and struck her where she stood, killing her instantly.

Most of us think to look both ways for traffic when crossing a busy intersection, my friend observed, but who would think to look both ways when moving from the washer to the dryer?

No matter how much you own, no matter how much honor, position, or pleasure you enjoy, death will take it away. As one of my college professors once said,

"Hell knows no aristocracy." There's no first-class, no special privileges there. The psalmist seemed to be saying this when he penned the words, "Do not be afraid when one becomes rich, when the glory of his house is increased; for when he dies he shall carry nothing away; his glory shall not descend after him" (Psalm 49:16,17).

In the face of death, we are all on equal ground. In supreme irony, death is one of the few certainties of life.

Some people believe that if you know the Lord, the death of a loved one shouldn't be a difficult thing. They want to think that God in His grace will insulate them from all grief, pain, and loss. But death comes to the believer and unbeliever alike, and it hurts just the same. If we try to pretend it doesn't, we only hurt more.

Some insist there is a prescribed way to feel about the loss of a loved one, but frankly the proper response is *your* response. Back in John 11, Mary and Martha grieved deeply over the departure of Lazarus, and Jesus never reprimanded them for it. In fact, Jesus Himself wept over the death of His friend, even though He knew He'd raise him from the dead. There's nothing wrong with hurting over the death of a loved one—as long as you do so with hope.

And hope is exactly what Jesus gave His friends in Bethany.

I am the resurrection and the life. He who believes in Me, though he may die, he shall live. And whoever lives and believes in Me shall never die (John 11:25-26).

Jesus asked Martha, *"Do you believe this?"*

In an earlier encounter with the final enemy, Jesus

was with Jairus, a leader of the synagogue, when that young father first got news of his little girl's death. It must have hit Jairus like a two-by-four across the back of his head. It must have sucked the air right out of his lungs. He might have crumpled into the dust...but then he remembered who happened to be standing next to him. In that moment of tearing fear and loss and grief, he looked into the eyes of Jesus Christ, and Jesus didn't blink or flinch.

"Don't be afraid," He said gently. "Just believe."

For people in the first century, Mary and Martha and Jairus included, death *was* a fearful thing, a frightful unknown, a black and terrifying mystery. In those days they called it "going behind the curtain."

Jesus, however, was about to remove death's horrible mask, and neutralize its paralyzing sting. Within scant weeks of those encounters, He Himself would die, be placed in a tomb, and go "behind the curtain." When He came out of that grave, He threw back the curtain, shouted eternal victory over it, and destroyed "him who had the power of death, that is, the devil, and [released] those who through fear of death were all their lifetime subject to bondage" (Hebrews 2:14-15).

No, the fact that you believe in God won't keep death from knocking on your door. But what you believe will be instrumental in helping you walk through it.

So I ask you: Do you believe this? Do you believe in God? Do you believe the Lord Jesus died for you? Do you believe He is the Resurrection and the Life?

It's little wonder that Jesus said, "Let not your heart be troubled." Don't be worried about life or death. When you know your ultimate destination, life itself becomes more peaceful.

I heard about a seventy-eight-year-old preacher who received a call to become the pastor of a small congregation in California. He hadn't been there long when the people began to murmur and complain about his preaching and pastoral care. He wasn't what they'd expected. He wasn't very impressive. He didn't work long enough hours. He didn't have much charisma or pizzazz.

Some of the people decided to mock and belittle him during the services, hoping he'd take the hint. As he was preaching they would sit in the back of the little country church, talk, make noise, and do anything they could to distract him. When that didn't work, they decided to starve him out, withholding their tithes. Finally, before they could fire him, this gentle shepherd, because of his love for the church and the gospel, chose to resign.

As he left the sanctuary the morning of his resignation, two young seminary students approached him.

"Pastor," they asked, "what are you going to do? Where are you going to go? You have no family. You have no money and you have no home. Where will you go?"

The godly old preacher looked at those two young men and said, without hesitation, "I'm going to heaven."

"Well, we know that," they said, "but where are you *really* going to go? You have nowhere to turn and no one to help you."

Again, he looked at them and said in a voice filled with joy, "I'm going to heaven. And the fact that I'm going to heaven makes these times of temporary hardship seem insignificant."

You can view death only one of two ways. If you're a believer, death is the beginning. If you're an unbeliever, it's the end. It's the end of every dream, every desire. It's the end of relationships, joy, and pleasure. It's like driving in the country, enjoying the ride, and coming to a dead end. It's the end of life.

Death is hard enough to experience, let alone to try and explain. One of the most difficult times in my ministry was when one of the young moms of our congregation passed away. It was a shock, and it came with suddenness and deep pain.

This precious family, with three children, was now without a momma. I was asked to talk to the children, to explain what had happened and try to answer any questions they might have had.

I had no idea they would ask such straightforward things. The little girl sat there with her pretty pink dress and pigtails and put her head down and began to cry. I got up from my chair went over to her side, and got down on my knees next to her.

"Honey, what's wrong?"

"I miss my mom," she cried softly. "Someone told me she was never ever coming back again." She knew her mother was in heaven, but she'd rather have had her mom at home.

"She's with the Lord in heaven," I said. I wanted to tell her all about God's house, her mom's house, and heaven itself.

But she had another question. Between sobs that tender little voice said, "How did my mom *get* to heaven?"

"Well, uh, um, you see," I stammered around—and then remembered a simple explanation I had heard. I said, "Can you ever remember falling asleep in the living room watching TV, eating cookies, and drinking milk, and then waking up in the morning in your warm bed? How do you think that happened?"

She thought for a moment. "I don't know," she said.

"Well, let me tell you," I said. "When you fell asleep, your dad, who loves you very much, came and picked you up in his arms and carried you into your bedroom. He put on your pajamas and tucked you in bed, pulled the covers around you, and left you to sleep all night long.

"That's exactly what the Lord did for your mom. The Lord loves your mom very, very much and, when she fell asleep down here on earth, He came and carried her to heaven. She woke up in His house. You see! Your mom's so special to the Lord that He's fixed a place just for her."

You can't hide from death. You can't avoid it. But you don't need to be terrified by it. The psalmist said, "Though I walk through the valley of the shadow of death, I will fear no evil." As a shepherd, David knew what it was like to walk alone through the valley, and the potential dangers that lurked in the shadows. Yet he knew that the "shadows" could cause him no harm: the shadow of a bear can't bite you, the shadow of a lion can't defeat you, and the shadow of death can't conquer you.

When you know the Lord, death is only a shadow. There is nothing to fear. As one of my friends once said, "I'd rather walk through the valley of the shadow of death with the Shepherd, than in the lush green pastures without Him."

For the unbeliever who walks in this valley of death, there is no shepherd to guide and protect him. There is no light to brighten his path when he stumbles through the darkness. But for those who know the Lord, death is truly just a shadow. It's a defeated foe. And it is the doorway to heaven.

I read that in one year, 6,000 people are killed and 165,000 injured *just crossing the street.* Crossing the street these days is grim business. Maybe you get across, maybe you don't. But there is something you can do about it. You can look before you walk.

My suggestion is that you look to the Lord. He's the resurrection and the life, so we can say, "For to me to live is Christ and to die is gain."

No, there is no "hiding place" on earth. But if you know the Lord, *every* place is safe. That's why David could sing, "I will fear no evil, for You are with me." For the believer, death is not a tragedy, but a triumph. The worst that can happen to you is the death of your old body; and to be absent from that body is to be at home with the Lord (2 Corinthians 5:8).

When the great preacher Jonathan Edwards warned his listeners of their imminent encounter with eternity, there were no lumbering trucks nor racing cars to watch out for. Crossing the street was a relatively safe endeavor in those days. Yet death stalked its prey and claimed its victims unexpectedly through other means. The way to prepare for such a tragedy was to do what Edwards counseled so long ago, "PREPARE TO MEET THY GOD."

I heard the story of a woman caught in a frightening storm in the middle of the Atlantic Ocean. She had kept all the little children on board from panicking by telling Bible stories. After finally reaching the dock safely, the ship's captain approached the woman, whom he had observed in the midst of the tempest.

"How were you able to maintain your calm when

everyone feared the ship would sink in this storm?" the captain asked. As she looked up, he noted the same quiet peace in her eyes that she had maintained throughout the journey.

"I have two daughters," explained the Christian woman. "One of them lives in New York, where this ship is bound. The other lives in heaven. I knew I would see one or the other of my daughters in a few hours. And it really didn't matter to me which one." She was safe in a storm.

Are you safe?

Dave Culver, one of the great men in our congregation, came to me one day with a story about his daughter, Diane. Diane Culver is a precious young woman who happens to be afflicted with Down's syndrome. She lives in a group home in Salem, Oregon.

Diane's mother was very ill, dying of cancer, and the situation was not improving. Dave decided to bring Diane home to Portland so she could visit her mom. After a short visit, Diane went back to Salem, but was very disturbed and emotional about the state of her mother's condition.

Upon arriving at the group home, Diane asked if she could meet with Mary, a professional counselor for disabled people. Mary immediately noticed that Diane seemed troubled.

"What's wrong, Diane?"

"It's my mom," she answered. "I'm afraid my mother's going to die."

As Diane proceeded to talk to the therapist about her mom, she suddenly stopped, looked off into the distance, and a peaceful, serene look spread across her face.

"What is it Diane?" asked the counselor.

"Quiet!" she said, holding up her hand. "Someone is talking to me."

For a minute or so, not a word was spoken, and then the counselor finally asked, "Who is talking to you?"

"It was Jesus," Diane answered.

"What did He say?"

"He told me that He was going to take care of my mother, and that everything would be all right."

From that moment on, Diane's demeanor changed. Her emotions were completely under control.

Some time later, Diane came back to Portland and was with the family when her mom, Anne, passed away. The night of the funeral, the house was filled with people. There were people sleeping everywhere, so they put a cot in her dad's room and she slept there.

About 2:30 in the morning Diane woke up, rose from the bed, and opened the door to the bedroom. Dave woke just in time to see her coming back into the room. He gently asked her what was wrong.

"I saw a bright light," Diane replied. "I thought someone left the TV on or something in the other room."

Dave was puzzled. Everyone was asleep; there was no TV, no light on anywhere in the house.

"What light?" Dave asked.

She looked at her dad and said, "It was Jesus. He told me that Mom's with Him now, and that she's just fine. He said she was His to take care of."

With that, Diane went back to bed and quickly fell asleep.

People often fabricate stories, create incredible

plots, just for publicity and attention. But this young woman had no motive to create such a fantasy. Even her counselors, who are *not* Christians, said there was no way for her to stage a scene like that.

In a life filled with Good Things and Bad Things, billions across our weary old globe think of death as the Worst Thing.

But isn't it just like our loving Lord to never send us anywhere He hasn't gone Himself? Isn't it just like Him to go into the shadow ahead of us? He went there and came back. He looked death in the eye and tied both hands behind our old enemy's back.

We'll still have to make the journey, but it's a very short way to go.

We'll still have to pass through the shadow, but we won't have to walk that way alone.

We'll still have to say good-bye to dear ones in Christ, but they'll be along before we know it.

We'll still have to walk around a dark corner, but just around that corner there's an ocean of light.

The Bad Thing, after all, is having to leave.

The Good Thing is that we're going Home.

CHAPTER TWELVE

The First Chapter

You had to pass through the valley of lingerie, take a hard right at hardware, and skim real fast through women's accessories.

And there you were...in the tricycle showroom.

In those days, state of the art was a low-slung plastic three-wheeler in fluorescent yellow and orange. My little son Mark and I stood there, holding hands, in awe of the trike-maker's craft.

Those sleek low-riding three-wheelers were all over the driveways and by-ways of suburbia. Ordinary tricycles were disdained as irrelevant artifacts of a bygone era. If you wanted to join the freewheeling neighborhood fraternity, you simply had to have one. Mark was already in line to receive one for his upcoming birthday.

But he didn't know that.

Sitting on the floor of the showroom—just waiting for someone to say, "Gentlemen, start your engines!"— were three or four different models. One was your basic, stripped-down, economy job; the Ford Pinto of tricycles. The next model up had a few flashy options. Streamers and decals and whatnot. And then, of course, there was one that had *everything*. It was loaded.

Mark gaped at it, wide-eyed. And in his mind I knew he was blazing down the lanes and avenues, sun on his back, hair flying in the wind. King of the cul-de-sac. Sultan of the sidewalk.

"Well," I said, "why don't you take it for a test drive?"

Mark didn't need any further invitation. He leaped on that little low-rider, raced down one aisle, screamed through the toy department, powered into men's wear, and circled back into the showroom. A few surprised customers felt the breeze as he went by.

He pulled to a stop in front of me, eyes sparkling, cheeks flushed with pleasure, poised on the knife-edge of hope.

"Well, son, what do you think?"

"Dad," he said breathlessly, "this one is *great*."

"Hmm," I said. "You know what I'm thinking, son?"

"What, Dad?"

"I'm thinking about Trevor."

There was a pause as he digested this. "Trevor?"

"You know. The little guy in our church. His mom and dad just divorced and he really doesn't have anything. I was thinking maybe we might buy this three-wheeler for Trevor. Wouldn't that be a wonderful gift for him?"

170

He just kept looking at me. Then his eyes lowered. He could still feel the power and glory of that trike beneath his little body. His expectations struggled mightily with the evident reality that the ultimate three-wheeler was not to be his. It was for someone else.

"What do you think, son? Do you think Trevor will like it?"

"Oh, Dad...he will really *love* it."

We bought the Dream Machine and put it in the trunk.

As we drove home, my little guy was very quiet. I guess I would have been, too. He had no inkling that we had already planned to buy an identical three-wheeler just for him. The very next morning Joyce went to the store and put money down so we could get it for his birthday.

Soon enough, this little story had its surprise ending. The three-wheeler meant for someone else was really, truly his. The dream that had been born and died in the same ten minutes was born again. He had his set of dream wheels and, better still, a hurting little boy named Trevor did, too.

To Mark, it was all a wonderful surprise. But his mother and I weren't surprised at all. We knew it all along. We'd planned it from the beginning.

That's the way it is with our Father in heaven. He sees our sorrows, disappointments, and inner struggles. Because He loves us so, He identifies with our pain and cares about it more deeply than we can imagine.

But he sees more than we do. He sees the picture on the puzzle box while we turn the odd-shaped jig-saw piece around and around in our fingers. He sees the fine, strong character qualities we will develop in the future while we see ourselves muddling through perplexity and setbacks and sudden reversals.

> For I know the plans that I have for you," declares the LORD, "plans for welfare and not for calamity to give you a future and a hope (Jeremiah 29:11, NASB).

He knows what He is about. He knows what's in His own heart. He knows what He has planned for us. He knows what He intends to do.

Gideon saw himself as a hopeless coward, crouching in a wine press to hide from the marauding Midianites. But the Lord saw him as a mighty warrior, deliverer, and ruler over a resurgent nation.

Hannah saw herself as a second-class wife with a barren womb and an empty heart. But the Lord saw a baby in Hannah's arms, and a little boy who would become a mighty judge, and change Israel's history.

David saw himself groaning his life away in lonely isolation: a fugitive in the bowels of a limestone cave. But the Lord saw the son of Jesse seated on a throne with a crown on his head and an everlasting kingdom.

Elisha saw his mentor and dear friend ripped from his presence and carried into the clouds by a fiery chariot. But the Lord saw a mighty new prophet in Israel with a double portion of Elijah's spirit.

A young Galilean couple saw the incredible embarrassment and humiliation of a wedding party with no refreshments for honored guests. But the Lord saw six empty stone pots—and some well water that would become the talk of the town.

Mary Magdalene saw a corpse slumped on a cross,

the agonizing death of her dearest hopes and dreams, and then the final indignity of an empty, plundered tomb. But the Lord had a Sunday morning surprise up His sleeve.

And you, dear friend, see Bad Things hammer into your life in quick, painful blows, or seep into your life like fog, obscuring your vision and chilling your hopes. You may feel you've reached a Last Chapter in your life. Like you've turned the last page, feeling let down by a disappointing ending.

Don't you believe it. There are more pages to turn. There are more surprises ahead, whether here on earth or just down the road in our Father's house. And all *those* things are very, very Good Things.

Let's call it a beginning.